How to Buy a Property in Spain

E-Book

(El Pequeno)

Felix Joseph

Forward

If you have downloaded a Spanish property guide from a law firm, currency Exchange Company or
Real Estate Company you will have read what is essentially a sales brochure.

This book is not the same type of document. This is the short version of the book which exposes the buying process in Spain, warts and all in an attempt to help you complete the buying process safely and without financial loss or stress.

This book is going to tell you everything that they won't, what you really need to know and look out for when buying a property in Spain.

Why I wrote this book

As a bank repossession specialist about a 3rd of my clients came from people who had tried to buy a normal property in Spain (via the real estate process), and had been taken in by an unscrupulous estate agent, misinformed, misadvised , not protected by lawyers who did their job (which in their mind is following the law and not the protection of their client) , lost over 10% of the purchase price often between 30 and 80,000 euro), and were then left looking at buying a knock down price Spanish bank repossession property as the only hope of keeping their Spanish property dream alive, (which is in fact by researching Spanish bank repossession properties is how they found me).

One day I began to think, If only I had got to them sooner, if only I met them before they started rather than at the end of their property journey. I know I could have helped them to buy that property safely. I know I could have saved them the loss of tens of thousands of pounds. I know I could have saved them life changing and life challenging amounts of stress and been paid handsomely for my efforts. It is actually these true stories which inspired the writing of this book.

A note to the reader

In order to save time this book has been written with the assumptions that you are from the UK. Over the years I have had clients from all over the world but the majority of my clients have been British. It is also assumed that you are buying a property with a Spanish mortgage as the majority of my clients do. This does not mean that this book will not apply to other overseas nationals, naturalized Spaniards or people who are buying in cash. As you go through the book you will see that most of the lessons, advice and insights apply to any buyer from anywhere. So if a section does not apply to you please ignore it as appropriate, I am pretty sure that the next one will.

Chapters:

1. Step 1...It's not what you think

Most people think that finding your perfect property in Spain starts with an internet search for the type of Villa or Apartment that you want but this is not the case.

In truth the old adage applies, Location, Location, Location (or ubicacion, ubicacion, ubicacion as we say in Spain), applies.

Frankly there is no point in looking at houses, Villas or Fincas no matter how appealing they are unless you already know the area you want to live in, so your Spanish property search starts with area.

Now for some of you this will be easier because you already know the area or at least have a good idea of the Coast or town you want to live in, you may have already visited there for many years on holiday. If this is you, then your job is simple, you have already narrowed your search down to a few towns or even one town, now all you have to do is find a good consultant or agency to help you and start looking for the type of property you want.

But for some of you this will be a lot more challenging, maybe you have no idea where in Spain you want to live. Maybe you've never been to Spain before but are just sold on the Spanish ownership dream.

This is not a problem, but it will be a lot easier for you and your agent if you have already done some research and have narrowed down your areas of interest.

I have had lots of clients who come to the Costa del Sol because they saw a house they liked and after looking at the house and staying in the area for a few days decided they actually wanted to be on the Costa Blanca.

Again, this is not a problem, in fact it is an essential part of the buying process but obviously the more research you do will be the less time and money you waste flying to Spain to visit the wrong areas.

So do your search on the internet first, there are now so many internet resources with reviews and recommendations of areas and places that you can get a good idea of any area in Spain before you get there.

Top Tips for finding your area

- If you have been to Spain before think of the places you enjoyed the most.

- If you have never been to Spain, think of what you want most from your Spanish property and research the areas with those features and attractions
- Do as much internet research as you can
- As your friends and use online reviews

2. Find your agent

In most books this chapter would be finding your property and that would be true here if it really were the next logical step but unfortunately it isn't. I mean don't get me wrong we all love to browse at Spanish properties whilst we are still in the 'wouldn't it be nice or maybe stage of the process'. But once you make up your mind to that you want to buy in Spain the most important next step you need to start looking at is who is going to help you through the process and who is going to help you find the property you want.

Now of course in the technological age we live in, with the internet you can find the property yourself but the problem is that many of the properties you find could be listed for sale by a bad agent and a bad agent could be your downfall.

I have seen smart buyers walk away from their dream home because they were canny enough to work out that the agent was untrustworthy, so finding your dream property being sold by your nightmare agent is more trouble than it's worth

'Ok', I hear you ask 'so my next step is to find an estate agent?'Err not exactly.

Before you find your agent: Why you need a property consultant

I have a Mentee a very brilliant Real Estate Agent called Pepa
At one of our informal mentoring sessions we discussed the role of a real estate agent she said to me and I paraphrase, the problem with estate agents is that they list properties for sale in which instance they are working for the seller and then they offer those properties for sale on the market in which case they are working for the buyer so in the end they don't really know who they are working for, and she finished off in very Spanish fashion with the words 'The agent really should know who they are working for'.

This for me was a light bulb moment and I have come to call this the Pepa problem, (I did tell you she was brilliant).

I found out much later that America had also solved the Pepa problem by not only legally requiring all real estate agents to be licensed (ok I knew this bit already), but having them license to work for either buyers or seller so that a property transaction was the meeting of two representatives, one for the seller and one for the buyer each defending the interests of their client (that bit I did not know).

So it with this understanding that I suggest the first thing you do when looking for a property in Spain is to find a property consultant. Yes unfortunately they are few and far between but as the example above shows they solve the Pepa problem and bring you closer to the safety and security of the American system.

Yes they will cost you and extra 1% on the cost of your purchase but that is an insurance policy against the hundreds of thousands in bank debt and your own hard earned cash which you could lose buying in a country you know little about without one.

I understand that this might need a little more explanation so in doing so, allow me to go back to the Pepa problem to elaborate.

If you have bought a house in the UK (or even if you haven't), I'm pretty sure that by now you will have worked out that Real estate agents are businesses and not charitable organizations. The number one aim of a business is to make money (this is at the very least because most businesses especially those with shareholder aim are to maximize profits) or at the very least need money to keep the doors open.

Ok so with these facts established the Pepa problem comes into focus.

In Spain the Real Estate agent is paid by the Seller, so as a buyer they are not representing your interests.

It never ceased to amaze me how many buyers think themselves very clever by taking advantage of this system without realizing that it actually works against them, because in life you get what you pay for. If the real estate agent is being paid for by the seller and you are paying nothing for the real estate agent then with regards to service and protection from the real estate agent nothing is exactly what you will get.

What you need is a property consultant or representative who you pay to ensure that he is working on your behalf and working in your best interest as opposed to relying on the real estate agent who the seller pays to ensure that he is working in theirs

Add to this the fact that the worst agents do not even work in the sellers' best interest, they, like all businesses fulfilling their primary aim (which is to maximize profits) should, work in their own best interests. As a middle man this really is very easy to do and in short looks like this. The seller gets less than he wanted for the property and the buyer pays more than he needed to for a property that was not the best fit with an unsuitable mortgage product because it came from the bank who paid the estate agent the highest kick back for your business. But hey, the good news is that the real estate agent made a sale, Ching Ching!!!!!

Now many of you will think that your protection is the job of your lawyer and this is to some extent true, but only to the extent of your protection under the law.

It is not the lawyers job to know if you are getting into a good deal or a bad one, just to protect you if any elements of it are illegal.

They do not negotiate on your behalf and this is a good thing because the tunnel vision many of them need just keeping up with changes in the law would make them terrible at it if they did. So although you need a great one on your team, this is not work for your lawyer. This is a job for, pause, your Property Consultant.

So, how to solve the Pepa problem? Believe it or not the Americans have got it right.

Business is war and you need a representative whose job it is to look after your interests and fight for them against the interests of others, that being the interests of the seller, lending bank and the estate agent.

Would you spend 6000 pounds to save yourself losing 100,000 or worse being put into 100,000 pounds worth of bad debt?

If the answer is yes then before you buy a property, before you exchange at private contract, before you make a reservation agreement, in fact before you even book to go viewing properties, you need to find and employ a property consultant.

Your Property Consultant

You will see a lot of real estate agents use the title Property Consultant but this is not the case. These guys are really just real estate agents who wanted something different and appealing to put on their business card

A consultant is by definition impartial, they may recommend real estate agents, (I mean they are best placed to, they will have worked with many and will know which ones specialise in which geographic locations or which types of properties),

The way to tell the difference between a real estate agents (basically a salesman for real estate), and a Property Consultant is simple. One represents all of your interests as a buyer and is paid by you and the other only sells property and is paid by the seller.

So don't take their word for it, they have every reason to lie and plus Spanish Property Consultant sounds way cooler than real estate agent, a term that many of us by now have reason to be wary of so look at what they do, look at the service they provide, that will tell you what they really are.

What your property consultant will do for you?

A good Spanish property consultant will simply do everything. He is your Spanish Property problem solver.

In the simplest of terms your property consultant is your right hand man or woman. He is your best friend helping you to do a thing that you know nothing about but he has done one hundred times and knows the ins and outs of. He knows all of the tricks, tips, recommendations and contacts and will help you to avoid pitfalls, problems, financial loss, stress, frustration and deceit.

You employ him for his expertise, knowledge, experience, contacts, patience, hard work and honesty. You pay him well and in return he helps you with every aspect of the purchase process, from the initial area research and finding the right estate agent for you, right through to successful completion at notary, and connecting the utilities to your new home, furnishing and any renovation work required.

You may not have heard of the term Property consultant and many real estate agents and lawyers will not have either, but that is because they are only focused on their little bit of the puzzle. A property consultant looks at the whole picture and helps you to complete it with minimal loss or mistakes.

As you will read in this book the financial benefits of employing this good friend run into the hundreds of thousands, the lifestyle benefits of the advice and protection from this good friend are the difference between getting your dream property and financial ruin, and the health and mental wellbeing benefits are priceless.

The Spanish Property Agents Network

Most importantly due to a number of real estate agent systems, most real estate agents register almost all of their properties on the same systems which other real estate agents have access to. So rather than thinking that you can only buy your dream property with the crap agent who listed it the opposite is true. You can actually buy almost any property in Spain with any agent so finding the agent you want to work with is key. Once you have selected your agent, you could actually find your own property and tell her which one you want to buy safe in the knowledge that she will help you rather than hinder you in the process and as the sales commission is usually paid by the seller this will come at no extra cost to you.

Finding your Agent...Again

OK so now you have found your area or at least narrowed it down, but don't book your tickets just yet because when you get to your area you're going to need someone to show you around.

Now I know traditionally a lot of people have just gone to the area and walked the streets popping into estate agents offices to see what local estate agents have available but this has its down side. Firstly, you might not find any agents depending on how remote the area you are looking at. Secondly, the local real agents (you know the ones with the high street offices close by to your dream area), might not actually be good ones so you are limiting yourself to what you find and who you work with when you arrive.

With the internet and social media you now have a greater chance of finding the agent you want to deal with, one who has;

A proven track record and Understands your needs Understands your values, cares about your requirements, Listens to your time constraints respects your budget and who is willing to make his or her money by achieving your goals as opposed to their own

An Important note

I talk a lot in this book about bad, poor or criminal estate agents not because the property industry has more lazy, inept or downright dishonest scoundrels than any other industry (ever tried to hire a plumber), but because in my job as a Property consultant and in trying to protect my clients I have come across a lot of them and the intention of this book is to help you to avoid them.

You know the type of real estate agent I mean, the one who has decided which property they want you to buy (because it has the greatest commission for them), even before you get off the plane or misinforms you, misleads you or downright lies to you about any or all aspects of a property or the process just to get you to agree to a sale.

Finding a good agent can be a mine field so we suggest that you do not leave it to chance.

Don't go looking for properties and then just work with the real estate agent who has the property you like advertised

As a said before, it is a little known secret (Not anymore ha-ha), that there is an agent's network and most agents have access to most of the properties available for sale on the coast so you are not tied to a bad agent just because they advertise a certain property for sale.

A better plan would be to find the property you want, make a note of it in a folder or online and then work with your Property Consultant to search for the agent you trust, like and believe will give you the best service.

Once you find the right agent, you can then send her examples of all of the properties you liked the look of. She will more than likely have access to exactly the ones you want and even if she doesn't, if you have chosen well, she will be able to find you something similar.

Do not go into the biggest real estate agent with the biggest advertising budget assuming that these things make them trust worthy or more efficient.

If any of you have been invited to a presentation by a Con man or a Scam company in the past, you will have seen that they book the 5 star hotel as the venue, they all arrive in expensive cars, the speakers wear expensive clothes all to make you assume that these people are successful and I suppose in one way they are. They are successful at using appearances to gain your trust and have made all of the wealth on display by convincing innocent people to work with them and then ripping them off.

Property is no different, so just because someone has a high street office or says we have been here since 1985 doesn't mean that they are trust worthy of even good at their job.

A prime example can be gleaned from the Spanish Property crash of 2007. All of the biggest real estate agencies with multiple branches along the coast went bust.

Many had not only been giving a poor service to customers but also had not been paying their employees commissions for almost a year. I personally know people who worked there and were left in financial ruins. The most famous of these real estate agencies shut up shop leaving hundreds of staff jobless and in debt, abandoning hundreds of customers half way through off plan purchases (which were never completed causing the investors to lose their money), and went off to America to try the same tricks where they were arrested within the first year of trading. I know that I mentioned that American really does have some things right with regards to real estate whilst discussing 'The Pepa problem' and this is proof of concept.

Similarly a Property Lettings agent (one of the biggest on the Costa del Sol), with multiple branches did the same leaving hundreds of keys to peoples apartment on the floor of their abandoned premises. I know this because my friend Miguel was the one who rented them the office space and I was there with him when he went to clean it up after they had left finding the bags of keys with no reference to who they belonged to which they left behind.

So you see bigger does not mean better quality or service, it does not provide you with safety or security. It might just mean that the company is better at attracting finance to buy big premises and fleets or cars, or have a bigger advertising budget to be the first Company listed in Google or appear on your Facebook feed.

So take a bit of time to research the quality of the real estate agent or better still get your Property consultant to do this for you.

So how to find the agent?

Social Media is a great place to start. Look for posts that tell you something about the agent their values, the company mission and not just the properties that they have listed

Also look for testimonials. I know that this is difficult as these might be false but although they can be faked often they not and they are still a good indicator so look for testimonials that are more balanced as opposed to just heaping praise in an way that seems unlikely for anyone for anyone to have written

Also ask for references, why because if the testimonials are real then some of the people will be willing to be contacted and back them up.

Ask around in Facebook groups and other such places where one agent will not be able to exercise control and other clients will be able to tell you about their experience

Use 'Trust pilot' and other types of rating agencies

Send them an email with a few questions.

But most importantly, call them up, have a conversation with them, get a feel of them

Don't just talk to the receptionist; a new con is to hire pleasant receptionists to hide bad service so ask to talk to one of the agents who will be touring you.

And as one contestant on 'Love Island' famously said, when it comes to making a decision between the head and the heart, Go with your gut (I know, you just couldn't make this stuff up)

This is why using a real estate agent just because of the property they have advertised is so dangerous. Because your gut feeling may be telling you to stay away but your interest in the property will make you feel forced to use them and this can be disastrous.

Remember most agents have access to most of the properties in Andalucía so there is no need for FOMO (Fear of missing out).

And even more importantly it's better to miss out on a great deal that comes with the kind of bad service which could potentially put you in financial or legal problems for years to come. It is actually better to get a good deal with great service as this will protect you and your investment during the purchase and for the future.

And Finally...

Do not take real estate advice from someone in a bar

Like most things if you have great karma there will be the one in a million case where a stranger in a bar recommends a fantastic agent to you but this is the exception to the rule.

If you take property buying advice from someone in a bar it is more than likely that you will end up on a program called 'Tonight', hosted by Sir Trevor McDonald talking about how you lost all your money in Spain

But it really does not have to be this way

Spain has robust legal systems and great real estate agents if only you take the time to look for them and use the same precautions that you would use when buying in the UK.

You wouldn't go to a town that you did not know and take financial advice from a guy in the pub at home, just like you wouldn't take medical advice from a stranger in a pub either, well at least I hope not, because if you did, you might not be around long enough to make it to Spain.

Top Tips for finding an estate agent

- Get a property Consultant first and use them to research suitable estate agents
- Do not focus on the property focus on the estate agent who will help you buy it
- Remember almost any agent can help you buy the property you want
- Do your research and see if they have a good reputation
- Call them on the phone to get a feel for them and see if they are right for you
- Do not take real estate agents advice from people you meet in a bar

3. Plan your visit

Areas of interest defined, Property types and budgets ball parked, Property Consultant engaged and Real estate agents short listed its finally time to start planning your trip to Spain to view potential properties.

First Matter on the agenda; Book accommodation in the areas you intend to buy.

You would be amazed at how many times a client has booked an apartment over 100 kilometers away from where they actually want to buy. This is like planning a shopping trip in London but booking your accommodation in Birmingham.

So no matter how cheap the accommodation is, think about it first because not only does it mean you get less from your agent, (I mean a 400 kilometer round trip to collect you from your apartment drive you to the area you want to buy in, drive you home and then drive themselves back every day for 3 days will not leave them with the level of energy they will need to be of good service to you), but also you are taking away an essential component of your tour.

Staying 100 kilometer from the area you want to buy in means that you will have less time to spend in your area of choice after the agent has left you for the day or before she has arrived. This means that you will have less time to get to know the area, wander around it, explore it, socialize, ask questions of locals and get a real feel for it this is the area for you.

This is a massive missed opportunity; in fact the ability to do this in person research away from your agent is arguable as important as the time spent with them so staying away from your target area is in effect wasting your own time and money.

So book your hotel in or near the area you plan to buy, even of it is a little more expensive, it will serve you more and cost you less in service and knowledge gained on the ground in the long run

Now that we have our hotel or apartment location here are few more key points.

Plan your transport

Is the agent collecting you from the airport? If not plan your transfers in advance.

Also if you are hiring a car which is a good idea, again sort this out in advance of your trip to get a good deal (or in the summer find no cars available at all), and do your internet research, there are some scandalous car hire companies offering cheap deals to draw you in only to scam you with high insurance, fake damage and exorbitant petrol costs.

Get an itinerary from your agent beforehand so that you can plan your days especially if you are meeting multiple agents, this will save both your time and their time and effort.

Also check the itinerary for duplicates for the same reason as above

Make any dietary requirements clear, although it is now a lot better than 15 years ago, do not assume that every restaurant has a decent vegetarian option or can cater for food allergies, so if the agent is buying you dinner make sure they know about your Gluten intolerance.

I once spent a terrifying time looking for a restaurant that could guarantee their food had no nuts to accommodate my clients daughters nut allergy, you'd be amazed how many waiters had no idea what was actually in the food and could give no guarantee for her safety.

Do not book your viewing trip and holiday at the same time.

If you book your property viewings as an appendage on to your family holiday you will most likely ruin both. You will frustrate your agent if he has to help you to pry your children from the pool in order to go to the viewing that he and others have given their work time to arrange. And you will not make the best decision in holiday mode, (que the friendly stranger in the bar buying you cheap beer with all the legal and property advice).

A property is one of the most expensive and committed purchases you will make in your life so give it the gravitas, seriousness and focus it deserves. Once you have the right property with the right legal's and mortgage in place, you will have plenty of time to bring the family out and do daddy or mummy bombs in the pool.

Lastly beware of all-inclusive IF's (Information Flights Paid for by Real estate agencies and Property Developers). This was all the rage in the early 2000s and as the market recovers it is making a comeback.

On Principle, we do not pay for our clients to come to visit properties. Why not? Well for the same reason Harrods does not send a car to pick you up to buy their Jewelry or Tesco does not buy you a bus ticket to come to buy their groceries. I am a customer too and when I want something I get myself to the shop to buy it I don't expect the salesman to collect me from my door.

Overall you will find that some companies who pay for your viewing trip will subsequently think that they own you which comes with an expectation that you will buy with them and buy with them now.

Paid for Information flights are like a creepy date where the suitor does everything for you and pays for dinner with the expectation that you are now beholden to them and your guilt will guarantee them something in return.

Similarly, do not use this type of agents ploy as a reason to be dishonest yourself by using them to get a free trip to Spain so that you can view with other agents. Firstly they have paid for you to be there so rightly or wrongly they will expect all of your attention and time whilst you are there on their dime. This will just cause an unpleasant and unsuccessful trip for you as you fight with the agent who has paid your fare and accommodations, trying to escape from them to be unfaithful with the person you are really interested in seeing.

The upshot of this is that you will have less time with the agent you really want to work with making your trip less successful and meaning that you might miss out on the property you really want because you just couldn't find enough time to do things properly in the time available to sneak away, so it really isn't worth it. Just be honest and pay to go, it will save you a lot of money and hassle in the long run.

So gentlemen pull on your big girls Bridget Jones pants, ladies put on your best big boys tighty whites and gender neutrals wear anything in between and then go and book your own flight, a hotel near your target area, transport to get to your agents offices and your own dinner reservations, just like you would if you were going to a conference for work or an away football match.

You will get much more from your trip and much better results in the long run

Lastly make sure that even if they are not bi lingual they work and engage with the Spanish. The best agents will work with Spanish providers and not just other Brits but more about this in subsequent sections.

Top Tips for Planning your visit

- Make sure your accommodation is close to the area you want to buy in
- Don't mix business and pleasure, your viewing trip is not part of your holiday
- Book your own flights and accommodation to make sure you are fully independent when you arrive and you can look at properties with whichever agent you want

4. Get your Ducks in a Row

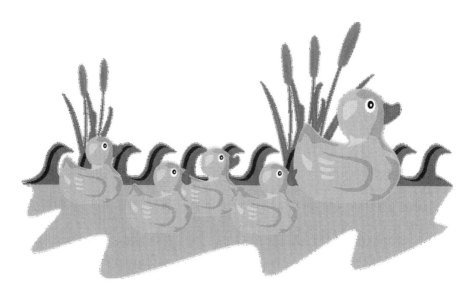

Now this is a difficult one to place because when I was investing in the UK we used to suggest that you get your ducks in a row before you went looking for a property so technically this should have been step 3 not step 4.

The only difference is that when buying a property overseas it is more difficult to finalize which agent, solicitor, mortgage broker and rentals agent because no matter how much of the research recommended in stage 2 that you do, you will probably still want to meet up with them before you make the final decision to give them your business, that is why this section appears here.

We do recommend that whilst you are looking for the agent you want to work with, that you investigate the law firm/lawyer and mortgage broker you want to handle your affairs as well.

Then you can arrange meetings with all of them when you finally come over to look at properties and this way even if you leave your viewing trip not having found the property you want to buy, it will not have been a complete waste of time because you will have found your property purchasing team which any property investor worth his salt will tell you is actually more important than any individual property purchase.

Documentation

This is an essential part of getting your ducks in a row and again something that bad estate agents will tell you not to worry about until you find the property you want to buy. This is because most estate agents do not think about anything further than the length of their nose and right before the tip of their nostril lays their commission.

So bad estate agents will only focus of one thing selling you the property, no in fact this is not true. Bad estate agents focus on one thing at a time, first schmoozing you to come over and use them for the Information flight, then to tour properties with them, then to sign a reservation form, then the private contract and then the actual sale. This single mindedness and tunnel vision means that they only consider other factors of your purchase as these factors affect them, so for example they do not mention a lawyer until you are ready to reserve because a lawyer will be necessary to for them to get to the next stage of their aim which is to make a commission.

What this means is that rather than helping you plan things in an orderly fashion which works for and benefits you, they rush you through the process pushing you to the next stage of their agenda leaving you to scramble and fill in the pieces you need to get there as you go along, and the documentation you need to buy is one of the first casualties of this approach.

In order to complete a property purchase in Spain you will definitely need;

Your passport

An NIE number (this is like a Spanish NI number and required for any major transaction in Spain)

But more importantly for you own safety and convenience you will probably need;

A limited power of attorney with you lawyer or Property consultant

If you are getting a mortgage your mortgage broker will need;

Your most recent 3-6 month bank statements
Your most recent 3-36 months pay slips
Your most recent P60
Your most recent credit report
A Nota simple of the property

(By your most recent I mean last issued or within the last 3 months whichever is closer)

Your lawyer will need from the seller or seller lawyer

The Escrituras (Mortgage and Title deeds) of the property

Your mortgage lending bank will need'

You completion funds transferred to you mortgage account usually at least four days before completion

Your Property purchase team?

Your team will help you to get the right property at the right price.

They will get the best mortgage for you at the rates that suit you and your financial circumstances

They will ensure that your reservation fees and deposit paid at Exchange of private contract are protected so you do not lose money

They will research your property, the seller and all of the legal aspects of your purchase to protect you

Ensure that your purchase and practices are in line with Spanish law to ensure that you do not get any unexpected fines or tax bills post purchase

Negotiate the right terms and conditions

Enable you to do the renovations properly and to cost

Resolve any problems which arise, particularly ones that you might struggle with due to language or cultural differences

Ensure that you have a stress free purchase and all aspects of it are done as efficiently as possible

As previously stated a good Property Consultant should be at the forefront of this team. Like a General instructing the armed forced on your behalf but if you cannot find a property consultant you will have to direct this team yourself.

So aligning those Duckies is actually more essential than finding you dream home, your dream home could become your nightmare purchase if you don't.

Your Lawyer

Meeting your lawyer in person is very important. This is the person who will be in charge protecting you legally, and like all things that rely on trust it would make sense to meet in person and get a good feel of not only the lawyer themselves but their operation. I have had so many clients out of a viewing trip who are quite rightly nervous. Of course at first they were nervous at meeting me and looking at properties in a strange land but once we had spent a day together, if I had done my job well that level of fear and worry disappeared. But fears regarding the legalities and technical complexities of the process remained.

This is why unless they already had engaged a solicitor I would always include a trip to one of my recommended solicitors, have her explain the buying process and legal ramifications and expectations to the potential buyer as part of their viewing trip.

We would make an appointment to meet them at their offices which would invariably end in 'taking a coffee' as the Spanish like to call it, at a cafe nearby.

I soon realised that once they had met the lawyer and had the whole process explained to them complete with all questions answered they released that final level of fear and apprehension and we could get on with the job of trying to find a property which was a perfect fit for their budget and aims and most importantly enjoying ourselves in the process.

But most importantly once they had this relationship with the lawyer, the relationship is theirs not mine. Just like in the UK once you engage a lawyer they work for you and nobody else (err except their legal requirement to report certain issues to the government or bank, but not the police hmm go figure)

The lawyer (like your Property consultant or Mortgage broker), is paid by you, they work exclusively for you. It is irrelevant that I introduced you to them, once you sign their letter of engagement they are beholden only to you (err and the bank and the government).

Now to a quick point of contention, yes it is true that Lawyers and even mortgage brokers pay referral commissions for the introductions of new clients.

In simple terms the lawyer that I introduce you to could legally pay me a flat fee or a percentage of the fees they earn from you for bringing you (the business) to their firm as opposed to another.

I appreciate that this makes some people uncomfortable and in the worst case scenarios their fears are well founded. Bad real estate agents choose the lawyers and brokers based on which ones pay the highest commissions (selling you off like slaves at an auction), rather than which ones are efficient, good at their job or will take the best care of their clients.

A good real estate agent will not, as the agencies he introduces you to reflects on his business.

I have personally stopped working with a number of businesses because they did not treat my clients to the same exacting standards which I apply. How could I do anything else, it would be like Gordon Ramsey serving you lunch and then sending you off to Burger King to get Desert (nothing against Burger king by the way, I am in fact a fan of their Rebel Whopper but not quite the same Michelin star standard I am sure you will agree).

So a good business will not recommend you to a bad one, lesson here start by researching and finding a good business to work with.

I personally have never taken a client to a particular law firm for a kick back. Not because I see it as wrong. No the reason I never asked for a referral fee is that the mission and vision of my business is one of excellence and as such it is important to me to recommend who I think is the very best That said I have paid estate agents for mortgage referrals, why not, why let the devil have all the best tunes and (as my intention is to do a good job), I know that by paying to get their business I was not only ensuring a steady flow of clients to my brokerage but I was actually paying to do the clients themselves a favour.

And lastly but most importantly, whenever you are 60% confident that you are no longer just speculating and you are serious that you would actually like to buy a property in Spain. Go to your Lawyer and sign a limited power of attorney.

This for me is an essential part of the process that so many people leave out only to suffer the consequences later. In fact this in my opinion is so important I will make a section for it

Signing a Limited Power of Attorney

Ok so let's start out with all of the reasons people do not do this;

- They are not advised to
- No one explains the benefits if they do
- No one explains the potential problems and inconvenience if they don't
- No one explains the reasons why it will not be exploited

So let's look at these in turn;

You are not advised to.

Poor agents do not advise their clients to sign a limited power of attorney because your legal representation is not their current concern; it is to use our previous analogy beyond the end of their nose. On your viewing trip their only concern is that you don't get back on that plane before you have signed a reservation contract and anything beyond that (no matter how inconvenient or how much difficulty it might cause in the future) is an afterthought.

They know that as a new buyer in a foreign country looking for people to trust, the suggestion of signing a power of attorney to 'Johnny foreigner, the lawyer' could make you nervous or suspicious again reducing their rapport with you and making it more difficult to sell (a bit like telling you that all you will need is 10% of the price to pay for the costs of purchase when they full well know the actual number is more). Why would they do this, well because weak characters don't tell people uncomfortable truths, they just kick the can down the road hoping that by the time you notice or find out you will be so far down the process that you will have no option but to continue and however you do this is no longer their concern (and once they've got you to sign an exchange at private contract and pay your 10%, they are right).

No one explains the benefits to you.

Ok well then allow me to. Very few of us are able to book time off of work, get an overnight minder for the kids or the dog and hop onto a plane to a foreign country just to sign some documents or arrange for a utilities company to provide electricity or water to our apartment. Well if you don't sign a limited power of attorney this is exactly what you will find yourself doing. The mere fact that you are quite rightly nervous and perhaps even a bit suspicious of doing anything in a country where you do not know the laws and norms will often (unless guided otherwise), preclude you from doing this earlier. But once you have bought the property you will almost certainly do this later if only to allow your lawyer to connect said utilities or your property management agent to represent you in the case of a leak etc. So since you are going to do it anyway why not just take the time to find a lawyer you trust and get the benefit of doing it in the first place. Because if you don't...

The problems of not doing one

Ok let me be clear, it is not essential to sign a limited power of attorney and yes thousands of overseas buyers have bought properties without one. But you are not here to be like them. Thousands of buyers have also had problems and stress throughout their property purchase and a few thousand no doubt have been ruined by it. You are here to avoid all of that and my job it to tell you the most practical steps to take to complete your Spanish property adventure safely and securely and stress free.

I have as a property consultant, real estate agent and mortgage broker been in the middle of so many instances of buyers stressed up to their eyeballs because they need to book last minute flights (last minute flights are usually the most expensive when the destination is fixed and dates cannot be moved), due to some administrative issue where something needed to be signed in order for the process to go forward.

Add to this the occasions where a problem occurs with one of the agencies who will be at notary, (Notary is where you go to complete the purchase of your property. Notary is the meeting of the buyer, the seller, the sellers' agent, the buyer's agent, the mortgage broker, a representative of the lending bank, a representative of the seller's mortgage bank, the Notary and often a translator in a room to complete the sale). At notary there are a lot of moving parts and it only needs one of these bodies to have a problem, lose a document or not have something prepared and the notary date may have to be rearranged. This is a big enough inconvenience if you already live in the country but if you are flying in to sign you will have to cancel your flights and that is if you are lucky enough for the problem to be spotted before you have arrived in the country or even at notary.

Yes it happens, all of the above mentioned parties actually get to the notary on the allotted day, at the allotted time and as the notary public leafs through the documents he frowns and turns to one of the people at the table asking for clarification regarding the piece of paper in his hand and If their answer is not acceptable to him he will tell the person to go away to get the issue resolved and dismiss the whole process until it has been.

So now we all pack our documents back onto our briefcases thank him for his diligence and leave. I mean how can we complain he is doing the job he is being paid to do, making sure that the transaction is clear, transparent, understood by both parts and above all legal. In this instance you will have to see out the rest of your stay and then fly back and book more flights for the new notary date fingers crossed that the same thing done not happen again.

This although unusual has happened to me on more than one occasion, there are just too many moving parts and even as a property consultant who communicates with every agency party to the transaction on your behalf I can only ask the questions, I can't physically do the work for them.

So as you can see, a lot of cost, stress and inconvenience can be caused by matters outside of your control if you insist on not giving the power to sign certain documents on your behalf to a solicitor or trusted adviser.

Ok so what about the risks, why won't this be exploited

For the same reason that your lawyer will not break faith with you on any matter (unless legally required to by the government and the law), because you lawyer, the one that you researched and is an active member of the Spanish law society, has spent 7 years studying to be given the license to practice and is not going to jeopardize that by being dishonest (They might jeopardize it by being incompetent but not dishonest).

Oh and if this isn't enough. The other reason the limited power of attorney will not be exploited is in the name. It's limited. Now don't get me wrong, business is fast moving and time is money so once you find a property agent or lawyer you can trust you can sign a general power of attorney to them which will allow them to represent your interests more effectively. But at this early stage, where you are just starting to trust, you do not have to give them that much power.

Sign a limited power of attorney that gives them the ability to do only specific things. If you are very nervous then wait until you have found the property you want to buy and then sign a limited power of attorney that allows them to only sign documents in relation to the purchase of that exact property.

This gives you the best of both worlds, the freedom to know that you will only need to travel to Spain to sign documents etc when you want to and the safety to know that whatever happens, changes or whatever mishap occur your interests will be represented and your ability to buy will not be compromised.

Should I use the lawyer recommended by the agent or developer?

Now this is where it gets tricky, lots of people would advise you to never use the solicitor or the mortgage broker recommended by the sales agent. The reasons for this are obvious, because if the agent is a crook, then use of his lawyer and broker will cement the fact that you will have the wool pulled over your eyes and be conned out of your money.

But on the flip side, if the agent is genuine then use of his recommended lawyer or broker will not only save you money but increase the efficiency of your purchase or even save a deal that would otherwise have been lost through incompetence or indifference. This is even more important the more complicated the structure of the deal. If there are any creative finance aspects to the deal you will need a lawyer and mortgage broker who specialize in this or at least understand it.

I cannot tell you how many times I have been doing a mortgage or a sale (acting for the buyer), who is buying from a seller using the family solicitor (you know the firm who has represented their family for the last 30 years specializing in Will writing or general law but have no idea regarding the use of creative strategies or up to date changes in the law etc), this can be a nightmare as I have found myself a lay man having to explain points of law to a solicitor just to get a deal done, this is not ideal.

So make sure your lawyers and brokers are specialist and one of the ways to ensure this is to take advice either via recommendation or from your property consultant.

Do you see now why step 2, finding your property consultant or taking time to ensure that you have a good real estate agent is so important? Finding a good one should the gateway to finding a good lawyer and broker too. I mean think of it logically, a good real estate agent will not be able to work with an inefficient or corrupt lawyer or broker. I myself have kissed a lot of frogs in this regard (and I mean a lot)

My mantra is anyone who gets in the way of me completing a deal has got to go. Arrogance in the legal profession is the bane of every property investor. If you are not already working in the UK property market just ask any investor there and they will tell you. Too many lawyers think that because they know more about the law than you, they know more about legally buying property than you, which if you are a property expert is very rarely the case.

I once had a lawyer lose me a 10,000 euros commission because she thought she knew better than me when she didn't and this was with one of the biggest law firm in the whole of Spain. Similarly after being told by two sets of lawyers that new laws in Spain meant that I could not legally remove a squatter my own research proved that the new laws could not be enacted retrospectively and so actually I could.

If you are a property expert (or your agent or property consultant is a property expert), it will be your/ their job to know better than your lawyer in terms of buying property. The Lawyers job is to help you define what is inside or outside of the law and in fact my best relationships with solicitors have been based on exactly this scenario. I go off and learn a new property buying technique from the USA or the UK and then call them for a meeting to ask if it is legal in Spain and if not how closely I could apply it.

The good ones usually say they have no idea (since they have never heard of it) and then go off the find out. That is how it works when it works well, two experts in their respective fields respecting each other's profession and working together.

So never assume they know more than you no matter how much of an air of self-importance they give off. They are specialists in their field not yours, and no matter how self-important they feel, they are there to do the job you pay them for (OK, rant over, arrogant know it all lawyers have lost me a lot of money over the years and yes I am seeing a therapist about it).

All ranting aside my main point is that even with the simplest purchase a poor lawyer can cost you time, money, cause you stress and in the worst case scenario lose you the deal so if you trust your Consultant or agent and they trust a lawyer based on experience of working with them it would probably make sense to give them a chance rather than rejecting them out of hand. But I return to my central theme you must first have a property consultant or really trust your agent (have I said that enough now).

Last point on lawyers, just like in the UK, Law school in Spain is extremely expensive and takes on average 7 years to qualify, And just like the UK there is a Spanish law society which monitors complaints against lawyers and can have them disbarred.

So just like in the UK you are much more likely to encounter incompetence or costly arrogance from a Spanish lawyer than outright dishonesty, for no other reason than in most cases it is just not worth their license to steal from you.

This is why big deals like off plans with developers are one of the few exceptions where I will look at the recommendation of a law firm more closely. Because if you are working for a developer who is providing you with hundreds of clients and you are earning hundreds of thousands of euros in fees from this one source, you are much more likely to bend and break the rules because at this point, for some it becomes worth it. The same goes for mortgage brokers too, so my advice in this situation is do a little more due diligence on the agent or developers recommendations before signing on with their chosen professional as in these situations you may really need an independent party to represent you interests an ensure that you are protected.

Your Mortgage Broker

Why you must speak to a mortgage broker before you view

Agreeing to buy a property and then looking for the finance afterward is by far the biggest and most costly error I see with people committing when buying property in Spain. This is a very dangerous version of putting the cart before the horse and I have seen it leave people in financial ruin.

Sorting out your finances is in fact the most important part of getting your ducks in a row yet so many people do not do it before they go viewing a property as if their ability to actually buy the thing that they are spending hours of their spare time and hundreds of pounds of their money to find is an afterthought.

The reason this is so dangerous , and I cannot stress the importance of this enough, is that human beings buy on emotion, all of us do, yes Mrs. Practical, you too.

So I know what you are thinking, you're just going to have a look; you're not going to actually buy anything. Well, I am not a high pressure salesman, I live by the mantra that the right property for you will sell itself, but I have lost count of the amount of people I have had climb into my car and say 'ok, just so you know, we are not going to buy anything on this visit, we're just here to look' (Add Leeds, Edinburgh, Sussex, London Accent to your taste). Only to walk into an apartment or villa and start to ask me what the procedure to buy it is.

So if this happens to me (a sales man so relaxed I might as well be asleep), imagine when you see your genuine dream Spanish home and have this emotion triggered by a agent telling you that 'there really is nothing else on the market like this right now' and that he has 'a second viewing on it in the morning unless of course the guy who saw it last week gets a green light from his mortgage broker upon which it will be gone tonight'.

Please note that this last selling ruse although it works as a form of pressure is actually a contradiction in itself. If your competition is waiting for a green light from his mortgage broker before he can safely commit to reserving the property, why are you then being advised to reserve it before you have first spoken to yours or even found one to help you?

But the dopamine in your brain spiked by planning your next year's family holidays has now overwhelmed all of your logic processing centers and you are rushed off to the sales office to pay your 6000 euro reservation fee or even (and catastrophically worse), 10% of the purchase price at exchange of private contract.

And as I will explain in depth (and repeat to the point that you think it's a misprint because it will seem like I have reprinted the section twice), this is a costly mistake that can lose you not only the property, but lots of money and possibly destroy your dream of buying a property in Spain altogether.

So, if I could shout (no I am not going to write it in capitals, Err Ok yes I am,

FIND AND AT LEAST TALK TO A SPANISH MORTGAGE BROKER BEFORE YOU GO TO VIEW ANY PROPERTIES!!!!!!!!

Putting the horse before the cart, (i.e. the correct way to travel from researching to buying), is to talk to a mortgage broker, (yes just like Property Consultants you will have to put some money upfront for the good ones) to make sure that they are working for you and not for the bank who is paying them the highest commission), and then you must give him a clear and 100% accurate overview of your financial circumstances. Your Broker will then go to his panel of lenders and return with the equivalent of a decision on principle (No, you do not get an official written decision in principle in Spain, one of the many strange and very annoying differences between the Spanish and UK mortgage lending systems).

This equivalent to a decision in principle will tell you how much money you can borrow. This added to the amount you have for a deposit and the 11 to 12 % costs of purchase will tell you overall how much money you can spend. This gives you the budget for your property purchase and now you know the maximum amount that you can spend, you can use this figure not only to do further research for yourself but you can tell it to your estate agent or property consultant so that they can ensure that their suggestions are within your budget.

Anything else is the equivalent of going to the super market loading up the cart with food, getting to the till and then looking in your purse to see how much money you have to spend.

So now you know how much you can spend and you have told this to your agent (the good one that you spent time researching), your agent will line up some properties within this budget and you are now able go out looking at properties safe from the financially ruinous effects of the hypnotic dream home dopamine kick, sleep walking you into signing a contract that your finances cant back up.

Tell your mortgage broker everything

When I was a mortgage broker in the UK I soon discovered a simple fact. Some clients tend to omit crucial aspects of their financial history from their fact find, and others just downright lie. This was very frustrating because we also worked with subprime lenders so the issue was never going to be could we find them a loan, just if we wasted a lot of time packaging applications for lenders who would ultimately reject them and then have to redo the whole process for a lender who would accept.

So in terms of getting your ducks in a row please follow my sagely advice, tell your mortgage broker everything possible and your solicitor only what they ask

Your mortgage broker will not judge you and it is his job to work for you to get you the loan, yes he does have to ensure that you can make the repayments on the loan, especially in Spain where some Spanish banks will drop a broker like a flaming stone if her clients stop making mortgage payments (yes that's right they make it the brokers responsibility so as the broker me and my business are the ultimate guarantor of your loan), but overall once satisfied that you can and will make the payments their aim is to find you the bank that you qualify with.

The solicitor on the other hand is duty and more importantly legally bound to not only work for you but work for the lender also. This means that anything you reveal to them they should tell the lender. It is at this point that I would like to remind you that just like in the UK, banks have no legal requirement to lend you money. There is not EU high court to which you can take a bank because they refused you a loan. Banks can discriminate as much as they want to, legally so if your lawyer reveals that you once had a mullet haircut and the underwriter hates fashion 'faux pas' that's your mortgage application in the dustbin right there. Ok this is an over exaggeration but the underlying point still holds true.

The banks literally try and get a feel of you and decide if they're going to lend you money as such, the less they know about stuff they don't need to know the better. Now I'm not talking about bankruptcies, CCJ's or unpaid loans here. If a bank refuses you credit because they did not like the fact that you were a speculative investor you have no recourse to complain or challenge their decision so if this does not come up in conversation don't bring it up. Immoral maybe, illegal, no and therein lies my point. So you know, just talk to your lawyer on a need to know basis.

What she doesn't know she doesn't have to tell which is one less obstacle in me getting you the finance that you want to borrow, and the bank wants to lend.

(P.S Not sure if I'm actually allowed to say this so I guess we will find out If I get in trouble and have to leave it out of subsequent re issues, hmmm lets see what happens)

In terms of what you reveal about your financial and personal circumstances;

- Mortgage broker everything, lawyer only what you need to,
- Mortgage broker, full disclosure, lawyer need to know basis,
- Mortgage broker 1, lawyers nil ,

Are you getting the point now?

Costs of Purchase aka Closing costs

This is another issue that is usually left right to the end which absolutely should be prepared for at the start. Every good businessman knows you start with the end in mind so before you commit to buying something you make sure that you will have the money to do so by the agreed purchase date.

Obvious right, well you would think so but as a property consultant and mortgage broker I have spent far too much time with people who, caught up in the romance and excitement of the fun stuff, viewing a property, looking at areas, designing the apartment, choosing furniture and planning family get together at their new holiday location, did not look at the essentials such as did they have enough money to actually buy the property.

At the time of writing the total amount you would need to buy a property in Spain is about 13% of the purchase price. This amount would cover the following things;

- ITP Government tax (similar to stamp duty)
- Land registry costs (to register your title)
- Notary fees (all property completions are conducted at Public Notaries)
- Mortgage costs
- Gestore costs

- Property Consultancy fee
- Mortgage brokers fees
- Solicitors fees
- Misc (inc Property Valuation fees)

You would think that ensuring you have enough money to cover this would be high on your estate agents list of priorities but again I refer you to my previous comments regarding estate agents agendas and nose length. You finding out how much money you need to buy is not on their agenda at this stage, getting you on a viewing tour or to sign a reservation form is.

In fact you knowing how much money you need to buy a property is never on a bad real estate agent's agenda until after you have signed the Exchange at private contract, at which point if they discover that their willful misinformation has left you with insufficient funds to complete on the purchase, their solution is to badger and bully you into finding the money. And if you do not find the money at least they get a share of the deposit you put down so all is not lost, well, all is not lost for them.

As a bank repossession specialist about a 3rd of my clients came from people who had tried to buy a normal property in Spain, been taken in by an unscrupulous estate agent, misinformed, misadvised, not protected by lawyers who did their job which in their mind does not include the protection of their client, lost over 10% of the purchase price (often between 30 and 80,000 euro), and were left looking at buying a knock down price Spanish bank repossession property as the only hope of keeping their Spanish property dream alive. If only I had got to them sooner, if only I met them before they started the buying process rather than at the end, I know I could have helped them buy that property safely, saved them the loss of tens of thousands of pound and been paid handsomely for my efforts. It is actually these true stores which inspired the writing of this book.

But I digress, in getting your ducks in a row make sure that you are 100% clear on how much money you will need to buy the property and that you will absolutely have it available before the completion date set on your exchange at private contract document. As the name of this document explains, it is a contract not a suggestion or a preference and if you are not ready to buy by that date you have forfeited all monies paid to the seller thus far.

So depending on what you are buying the costs of purchase will be approximately 11% - 13% for a re-sales purchase but still budget 12 - 15% if what you a buying is a new build. This is an overestimation but as I always say, 'budget for more than you need and after completion you will have change, budget for less and on completion day you will have problems'.

In simple terms if the property you are buying costs 100,000 euros you will need approximately 13,000 euros in purchasing costs to buy it. If it costs 200,000 euros you will need 26,000 euros to buy it and so on and so forth.

Please don't get lost in the stories I tell and miss the salient points behind what I am saying here. My central point is that you must make sure that you have this money or at least certainly will have it before you agree to buy anything and definitely before you sign anything.

So get your documentation right and make sure that you have the costs of purchase available before the completion date. I have seen so many cases where buyers are scrambling around in panic at the last minute to get funds in order to complete a purchase.

This is because with his eyes crossed and fixed firmly on the tip of his own nose, the bad real estate agents (you know the one you did not take the time to look into properly before you trusted), in the push to fulfill their own agenda and move the purchasing process along to the beat of their own drum will get their requirements met first and your convenience along with common sense and practicality will be the causalities.

You really haven't seen a look of horror until you've seen a buyer sat at notary who has been told that that he will need to find another 6,456.35 euros by midday to complete on his purchase.

So in summary,

Get your ducks in a row and make sure that you have enough money to buy before you commit yourself. Otherwise you may find yourself another cautionary tales from a property consultant who wished that he had the marketing budget to complete with the big boys so that he could have gotten to you in time to steer you in the right direction and helped you to avoid losing all that money.

Top Tips to getting your Duck in a Row

- Begin the process of getting the required documentation together
- Find a lawyer
- Sign a power of attorney
- Find a mortgage broker
- Start getting your mortgage documentation together
- Make sure you know how much money you will need to complete on the property
- Ensure that you will have this money available before completion day

Ok two more quick points I want to make whilst we are getting our ducks in a row. These could easily have been left until a later section, but since we are taking the pragmatic approach of organising all of the agencies before we come on a viewing trip so that we can meet and select the ones we want to work with from our short list I will include these here.

Your property management agent

This is a classic after thought and for too many buyers.

Unless their strategy is to manage the properties themselves most UK property investors have a property management agent and a lettings agent. I know these roles are often combined but I separate them here because they are actually 2 separate roles and in Spain this separation is more important than in the UK. In the UK most investors are advised to buy in an area local to their home so that they can manage the property themselves so unless they buy in another town, a property management agent is not required. Plus if the property is not their home then it will be a buy to let which means they will probably use a lettings agent many of whom also manage the property as part of the service.

But with an overseas purchase you are by definition not in your local area so you will always need a property management agent even if the property is for personal use.

You will need someone to check the property on a regular basis, for potential boiler leaks, if there is a storm to check for damage, just to visit it open it up and air it out, possible hold keys for yourself or friends when they visit, handle complaints, open the doors for deliveries and tradesmen.

All of these things are at best a huge and expensive inconvenience to you if you were to try to do them yourselves and you will have massive peace of mind once you have someone in place to handle these types of issues at the end of a message or a phone call.

Now if like most overseas investors you also want to rent the property out, either part time when you are not using it or as a fully blown rental property then this management agent service could also be part of your lettings agents work just like in the UK.

Either way you will need one which by now I am hoping you already know the mantra, you need to research one, get recommendations regarding one, phone or email one and then get a short list of potential candidates in place ready to visit and choose before you buy your property.

'Do I really need to spend time researching the management agent for my property' you ask. Well the client of mine who flew in for an impromptu weekend at his Apartment to find it occupied by holiday renters who he had not been informed about and was definitely not going to be paid for would probably say yes. He is not alone in this experience. Another client of mine had his Villa rendered useless after the agent didn't bother to check it after a flood losing him over 60,000 euros in summer rentals. Just like all other businesses there are good and bad property agents and if you are taking the time to read this book, I want to make sure that you end up with a good one.

Obviously this agent should be within the catchment area of your property to allow them to do their job with convenience and cost effectively (although this is not a hard and fast rule as a good agent willing to travel is better than a bad one who lives locally). But if you are choosing a local agent this makes it perfect as you can arrange to meet them when you come to visit your shortlist of areas on your first property inspection trip. This can be done as part of getting your ducks in a row, and as with all things if you want to take the pressure and stress from this process use your trusty Property Consultant to help you choose one.

Renovations and builders

Firstly just like in the UK, buying a property in need of a cosmetic refurbishment or even major works is a great way to get a bargain property.

Secondly you can get mortgage finance for a renovation project, it is a little more complicated but it is achievable, just like in the UK

The third and slightly controversial point is with regards to who you get to do the works.

You see, having lived here in Spain for 14 years and picked up the language (albeit only to a poor immigrant conversational level), I fully appreciate the problems faced by foreigners (and yes In Spain Johnny foreigner is you and not as so many expats seem to believe the other way around).

So if finding a reliable tradesmen in your home country poses a huge problem (and as I was a property investor in the UK I absolutely know that it does), then finding someone trust worthy overseas multiplies this problem considerably.
Well who can come to save us, is it a bird? Is it a plane? (Think 1960s Superman comic caption and image)

Yes, it's your friendly neighborhood web slinging Spanish Property consultant (yes I know I mixed my comic book metaphors)

Do you see now why we spent so much time finding a good one? Who else will have had experience with construction companies who have done renovation works to differing levels and know who is good or bad in a particular area? Again the best company might be in Glasgow but do you really want them travelling down every day to Warwickshire where your site is.

This highlights an aspect of finding a good agent I mentioned before, make sure that even if they are not bi lingual they work and engage with the Spanish so that they have an ability to get work done by Spaniards who are the majority of the workforce and therefore have a better chance of getting highly skilled good value for money tradesmen.

In finding a contractor for your renovation, like anything, you just need good, honest, impartial advice. Look on the internet for recommendations, Facebook, trust pilot, your lawyer, your mortgage broker, real estate agent or again if they have your trust the person with the biggest vested interest in finding you a good one is you property consultant .

The other option which I have seen people do to some effect with regards to their renovation workforce is to bring your own, kind of like a party where you don't trust your Spanish host to have your favorite of bottle of Plonk so in order not to have to slurp that foreign muck you bring a bottle.

The problem with this is 'Auf Wiedersehen pet ', approach is that although you win with regards to working with tradesmen you know and trust, you lose out in their ability to get access to the best resources, prices of materials and planning laws which will always leave them at a disadvantage when compared to the local work force and cost you more in the end.

So in summary, when buying a property which needs some renovation, make sure you do your research if you are going to find your own local contractors, make sure you are prepared and able to spend more if you are going to bring over your own and to simplify the process fall back on your Property consultant to get recommendations for the best tradesmen, preferably in your local area.

5. Finding your property

'Bloody hell, half way through the book and we are only just starting to talk about finding your property', Yep. This is what 14 years of helping people to buy property in Spain and more importantly helping people out of disastrous situations whilst trying to buy property in Spain has taught me.

Plus I know that you have been sneakily doing constant internet research, watching 3 year out of date re runs of 'A place in the sun' (and being totally misled as to the current prices), watching 'Bargain loving Brits in the sun' talking to friends and reading through the posts on Facebook groups, Quora and Reddit so I do not feel bad about taking so long to get here,

Now that we are finally ready to start looking for our dream home or investment vehicle, here are a few tips for your viewing;

Rome was not built in one day.
Act in haste repent in leisure.
The Hare lost to the Tortoise.
Are you starting to get the picture here?

You may need more than one trip

By now your own research should have helped you to narrow down at least the area or areas you want to buy in

If you do not know which area you want to buy in yet then use the first trip for area research not property research.

This really should be done on your own time and on your own dime so again don't take an information flight from a real estate agent in order to do this on the cheap.

At best he will feel cheated that he paid for your trip when you had no intention to buy and at worst annoy you with high pressure sales causing you to board your return plane home 6000 euros lighter with a reservation contract for a property you are not sure that you like in an area that you don't know very well and are not sure that you want to live in.

So you may find that your first trip is really just a 'Recky', a property reconnaissance trip to establish three things.

Area

First, visit the areas you liked the sound of.

Go in the day and look at the traffic, go at lunch time, go to the local beach, visit the local restaurants and Chiringuitos, if you are relocating check out the local school, if you are going to work in Spain, do the drive from the area to your new place of work. Essentially do all of the things you would do (or should do if you were going to buy a property at home)

Also visit the area at night to make sure that the local park that your kids played in with the other school leavers at 2pm doesn't turn into a drugs hang out after 10pm, or any other such unsavory behavior which only occurs in the evening. Get dinner, visit local attractions and make sure you have fun.

Visit your Agents

Second, visit your Property Consultant or agent. Yes I know you have already looked and asked for recommendations, you have sent and received emails and possibly even phone calls but nothing beats the gut feeling of knowing this is or isn't the right person to help you as meeting them face to face.

Also if you have narrowed down your selection to a shortlist of a few, then now is the time to make a final choice especially if you are hiring a property consultant to whom you will have to pay an upfront fee, or if you are stuck between real estate agents then at least narrow it down to the 2 or 3 you are going to work with

Meet your Lawyer, Broker and other agencies

Lastly use this trip to meet the other agencies you will need if you decide to go ahead and buy a property. These will include your mortgage broker, solicitor and property management agent. Far too often people leave this as an afterthought. The logic is that since they have not committed to a property, or even to definitely buying one in Spain at all, then this would be a waste of time.

The problem with this approach is that if they are with a pushy agent, then once they find the right property they will often find themselves railroaded into signing a reservation form and handing over their reservation fee quickly (you know because he honestly has a second viewing on that property later today from a guy who was very interested), before they have even chosen their solicitor.

So get ahead of the game, this duck should have been put in a row in the last chapter, at least research wise and now is the time to book an appointment and drop into their office or as we like to do in Southern Spain, meet up for a coffee and let them introduce themselves and find out if they are the one for you.

As such I suggest on your first viewing trip you reserve one day (not necessarily a physical day but a day's worth of work so maybe 6 to 8 hours over your 2 to 4 days), just for this. If you have a short list of potential agencies then make an appointment and meet them all. Select the Property Consultant, Mortgage Broker and Lawyer you want to work with, let them open a file for you and pay them some money on account so that they are ready to work for you the moment you find something that you want to buy.

Have a viewing checklist

Make a property viewing document. This is a document with property address, agent who showed it to you, area it is in and a list all of the things that you most want in a property. Print out about 15 to 20 of them and check off the points during the viewing of each property you see.

Sea View...

Check ✓
Garden space... Check ✓
Large kitchen...
In Andalucía... no bloody chance ✗

This will help you keep track of what you have seen and the differences between them.

Make sure you note down not just how they looked or the amenities they had but how they made you feel. This can be done easily with a happiness factor check box to be filled out when you leave

Happiness factor...8 out of 10 (this might be the one for you)

Happiness factor...4 out of 10 (this will be the one the estate agent wants you to buy and is still explaining the features of long after your soul has left the building)

It will also help that lunch time argument you will have with your partner or kids regarding which one had the infinity pool or the basement which they wanted to turn into a den.

A good agent may well have property sheets for you but these just have property details, they will not be personalised with regards to what you saw and what you felt, liked or disliked.

Also take pictures of each property or better still do a video walk through on your phone talking your way through them. Start by stating the urbanisation or street name and price before you walk in the door and then proceed to do a walk through explaining what you see and most importantly again how all of you feel about it.

In doing this don't be shy, it will be worth it when you go home and want to review your day and discuss what you saw.

I know many agents will try to get you to look at 10 to 12 properties per day but this is really unproductive. Yes you are making a big decision but too much choice leads to confusion, any good salesman knows that.

It is the salesman's job to listen to you, really listen and work out not just what you say you want, but what might actually suit you best from what he has to offer.

So a good agent who has been listening to what you have told him (providing that you actually know and are were telling the truth), should then do his job to research what is on the market and provide you with 5 to 6 properties per day maximum.

I have done tours where I have shown my clients only 3 properties at which point if I am not even close then I know that either I have not been listening or they have not been telling me the truth. Either way I take them for a drink to discuss where I am going wrong, hopefully get more insight into what they really want and then take them back to their hotel to enjoy the rest of the day whilst I spend my time constructively looking for a better fit for tomorrow.

Whist I'm here a quick note on telling your property consultant or real estate agent the truth. I mentioned before the mantra tell your mortgage broker everything and your lawyer on a need to know basis. So how much do you reveal to your property consultant or agent? Well again like your mortgage broker if you want to get the best from him you really do have to tell him everything.

Think of this like a doctor, if you don't tell them what's really wrong with you, how are you expecting them to help you

This is the reason why it is so important to interview and choose a consultant or agent before you look at properties. You will need to trust them and be comfortable enough with them to tell them 'the truth, the whole truth and nothing but the truth' or so help you God if you expect them to help you to get what you want.

You need to trust your agent, you need to tell them exactly what you want, you need to tell them how much you really have to spend, when you really want to complete, if you really want a mortgage or not.

If you don't trust them don't work with them, and like I said because most of the properties are accessible to most of the agents anyway you are better off choosing the agent whom you trust and can be honest with and giving him the information to serve you and in turn get you the property you want.

The second viewing

On a good tour where you have told the agent the truth and the agent has taken the time to listen, you will have had a shortlist of properties which actually interest you and plenty of spare time to hang out, revisit areas and do your own thing.

Of the properties you liked make sure you do a second viewing before agreeing to buy.

This is especially true of tours where agents give you a whirlwind tour of 10 to 12 properties per day. It is easy for a property to look good when compared to so many others (the old crap, crap crap, good one crap crap, a strategy I will discuss later), but does it still look good when viewed on its own. Does it stand out in its own right?

Before your second viewing spend a few minutes the previous night or same morning reviewing the property viewing sheets and video you took at the first viewing. Note all the good points that made you like the property, do you still feel the same way about them now? Note all of the bad points, did you just brush them under the carpet or are they really deal breakers?

Double check things you looked at before look for things you might have missed the first time. Try to envision yourself in the house or if it's for rental purposes, put yourself in the mindset of the tenant and do a walk through as them.

Buying to renovate and flip, do your second or third viewing with your builder (yes you have a builder, we got one when we got our ducks in a row before we started viewing remember). Get his opinion on the cost of the potential works and then do your own research (as well as asking your real estate) as to how much the property will be worth once it's been done up. Ask your mortgage broker if development finance is available (yes we got one of those too when we were duck lining), see if you qualify for that type of loan, do you need or can you get bridging finance?

If the first viewing is reading the headline, the second viewing is drilling down into the text and making sure you really understand what it says. Make sure you do, there will be a test on it later and the results will be if you bought well or lost all your money.

The second area visit

Much like the second property viewing make sure that you revisit the area, go to a different part of the beach, eat in a different tapas bar, get dinner in a different restaurant, go to local bars, night clubs, the marina, children's' activities, schools everything and everywhere that will affect your experience if you were to buy there

A great tip is to talk to locals or other holiday makers (if you can, I appreciate that this might be outside of your comfort zone), but if you can this is a great way to get their experiences and opinions of staying their (This is great source of information as; they are not making money based on the response to your questions so although subjective will at least be honest).

Take your time and make sure you can see yourself or your target end user living there and using the amenities

A word on Dodgy sales tactics

Firstly let me reiterate that just like any industry in real estate there are good and bad agents. Over the years I have known some very good ones but unfortunately, I have also met far too many unscrupulous property agents and it continues to break my heart to see how successful they are at selling properties to people which serve their needs not their customers

Of the many case studies I could use here the most useful tactic I can share with you is the jab jab jab right hook pause jab jab Knock out technique. Or with the less subtle agents this is the crap, crap, crap, property they want you to buy, lunch, crap crap pressure 'I have a second viewing on the only good property I showed you, tomorrow morning' so if you liked it you'd better move quickly, crap crap, let's go to the office and sign the reservation, order a bottle of bubbly and spend tomorrow at the solicitors and mortgage brokers.

As this suggests some agents will know what THEY want you to buy before you even get off the plane. In fact in the worst cases they know what they want you to buy before you even get in contact.

This is why this is so disdainful to me. There are two types of sales man; ones who make their money selling you what you want or need, and ones who make their money selling you what they want you to buy, regardless of your real wants and needs.

I am firmly in the first camp and have no time for my namesake in the second.

They make my job harder, they give sales and salesmen a bad name, they create unsatisfied customers, they are the reasons that my next customer arrives wary and untrusting due to a story they heard from a friend or saw on the news, they miss-sell to people and cause misery and hardship, they are lazy, greedy, slothsome and they are a disgrace to my profession.

So, returning to my point, the tactic.

They have a great deal with a developer who is offering 10% in commission to sell their overpriced or subpar quality apartments. This is a great deal for their business as it is twice what they would get for a normal sale, and then you walk into their office, on holiday, no research and wondering if you could view some properties.

You have no property consultant to advise you and very little knowledge of what is available.

Here is where we return to the Pepa problem. If you had a property consultant, they would work for you because working for you is how they get paid and benefit their business. If you luck out or do your research to find a real estate salesman who subscribes to the same sales philosophy as I do, then he will work in your best interest because based on his sales strategy, this is how he makes his money. But if you walk into the office of the salesman who sells for himself and not you, his decision will be clear. Sell you the property paying 10% commission above all others because that maximises the benefit to him and after all he does not work for you, you are not the one paying him. As the seller is the one paying him, he at best he works for the sellers on his books and in this scenario the developer is the highest bidder so he is going to sell you the properties they want him to.

And how does he go about this?

He will take you to four subpar properties in the morning, all of them good properties but not right for your needs. As he knows this he will rush you through them and as you are not very interested in them you will not mind. Then he will take you to the development where he is earning the 10% commission, spend more time there and make sure he wows you with the property. As this is the property you liked the most so far (by design), he will now take you for a tour of the immediate area to show you all the amenities and help you envision how great it would be to own a property there. 'Phew' he says 'it's been a long morning and I'm feeling peckish and since we are in the area of the property I want you to buy I just happen to know a great little restaurant in this area that you could use regularly if you bought here, lunch anyone?'

After lunch where he allows you to discuss what you have already seen, dissect the properties which were not suitable for you (he knows this already, he chose them that way), he will wait for you to confirm to him that the property he wants you to buy is the best you have seen so far and then restart the tour. Three to four more crap properties before the next pause for drinks and a toilet break. Let's review the day, hmmmm of all the properties I have shown you so far on this over loaded whistle stop tour you like the development that will pay me twice my usual commission the most, how uncanny. Well since you like it so much I am duty bound to tell you that the one you saw is; (choose from any of the following),

'The last one available'

'Has a second viewing on it tomorrow'

'Has been seen by a client last week who is just waiting a decision in principle from his bank before he reserves in tomorrow'

'Going up in price by 10% soon Etc etc, you get the jist.

Fear of missing out is a very powerful emotion and as you don't want to miss out on this great deal which will be gone tomorrow because of... (Please re read the reasons above).

He does you the favour of rushing you to his sales office or the office of the developer before you have seen a solicitor or spoken to a mortgage broker and taken 6,000 euros (or more) from your credit card to secure the property for you. What a great guy, well done, let's go have a drink to celebrate (Obviously this celebration is for him not for you because he got what he wanted, you didn't).

This is the reason why viewing the property is the 5th step in this book, because without the preparation of the first 4 steps this could be you. Having a celebratory drink to congratulate the agent who tricked you into the purchase of a property you didn't really want that does not fulfill your needs but made him a lot of money, Cheers!!!

Leave yourself spare time

And let me remind you to always leave yourself a day on your viewing trip for your own research. Once you book your own travel you are freed from any obligation or control. You go and come as you please. You can tell an agent they are overstaying their welcome without the pushback of knowing that they paid for you to be there. And most importantly, once you do see a property that you like, you can go back to the area on your own and explore it yourself at different times of the day to make sure that it really is for you.

And make sure that you leave that extra day to visit a lawyer and mortgage broker (I know I am repeating myself but I really want you to do this). In my opinion meeting your mortgage broker is a nicety, a courtesy and a good thing to put a face to a name or a voice but in this age of email and WhatsApp not such a necessity, whereas I have expressed earlier, meeting your solicitor is essential.

Top Tips for finding your Property

- Have a viewing checklist
- Do a second viewing
- Don't fall for Dodgy sales tactics

6. So you finally found your property

Hoorrayyy!!!!!! (I say this assuming that we are saying cheers to you finding something you actually want, not what the agent wants to sell you)

You viewed it,

You've been on a second viewing,

You went to the area all by yourself and you know that it is really right for you. You can envision yourself and your family in it.
If you've been lucky enough to have your children come over on the 2nd viewing they have had a look at it, and they have decided

that they like it, they love the patio and the local vibe. As the kids say, wow!!!!!! How lucky you are to have found what you want.

Now, it's very, very, very important to protect it and to make sure that you don't lose it. This is where the payment of the reservation comes in.

The Property reservation contract and the Exchange at Private contracts

Important Note: The general principles with regards to opportunity costs I explain here apply to both the property reservation and the exchange at private contract.

Like many things in Spain, reservation contracts and the associated payments are not homogenous, they vary. I've seen reservation payments vary from 500 euros to a bank for a bank repossession property to over 10,000 euros on an expensive villa.

That said the standard reservation payment is about 6000 euros on any apartment.

What is the purpose of the reservation? The reservation is simply for you to show your commitment to the buyer regarding your intention to buy their property and for them to show their commitment to you with regards to their intention to sell it to you.

You commit to the seller that you like his property and you intend to go forward and buy it (as long as it passes a few basic checks which shall be performed by your lawyer such as the seller actually has the right to sell it). Therefore you would like them to take it off the market and not show it to anybody else and they make this agreement with you to take it off the market for a specific period of time and not show it or sell it to anybody else.

It also locks in the price of the purchase so that you cannot try to low ball them later by changing your offer to a lower one and they cannot increase the sales price at a later date in an attempt to Guzzump you.

Great, but couldn't that be done with a handshake? Why do I need to part with my money?

Well, very simply the money paid at reservation is really just to enforce the commitment, (quite frankly, because words are cheap and money talks). The money for a reservation agreement (and indeed the following Private contract) is given not only to hold the property before completion of the sale but as a form of opportunity costs to compensate the seller for the time and sales opportunities lost in the event that you cannot go ahead and complete the sale as agreed.

Remember, you are now asking the person selling this property to take it off the market and not show it to anybody else. This means that if you have a change of circumstance or even worse, if you're not actually serious and you're just messing about looking at properties for fun they could lose out big time.

If you're not a time waster or a fantasist and your circumstances genuinely do change, it might seem unfair for you to lose this money. But in all honesty, even if you are being absolutely honest and genuine and your circumstances have changed. That cannot change the fact that the seller will definitely have missed out on the opportunity of selling the property to someone else in the time period it's taken for you to find out that you can no longer buy. As such, it's only fair that they are recompensed in some way.

So in understanding this, be very clear that in all but the most unusual circumstances, if you pull out of a deal your reservation fee and 10% deposit at exchange of contract will not be returned to you. It will either be deducted from the final purchase price when you complete on the property, or it will be kept by the seller as recompense for the opportunity costs of taking the property off the market for you and losing other potential buyers over the time period it took for you to find out that you could no longer buy.

Now that you understand this clearly, how do you make the reservation?

Reservation contracts pretty much follow this pattern;

They will always have your name and the seller's name, the property that you're reserving so there is actually clarity exactly what this moneys for, and which property has been taken off the market.

And we usually give you a certain amount of time between reservations to the next stage which is the exchange at private contract. As I said the reservation is really just a contract to take the property off the market and make sure that it is not sold to anybody else and it protects you, you time, your effort, the money spent and in many cases your dreams from the greedy antics of sellers and estate agents.

As a property Investor I have both been Gazumped (the seller selling the property he had previously agreed to sell to me to another buyer for a higher price), and had buyers pull out after I had taken the property I was selling off the market and refused other offers, so I have been on both sides of the argument and see both as 100% valid. Mess the seller around; lose your reservation fee and deposit. Try to Gazump the buyer and get taken to court for breach of contract and pay the appropriate penalties and the buyer's legal costs when you lose.

Even if the associated risks to you of losing your money are taken into account, the other major thing about a reservation contract, which applies more to investors, then lifestyle buyers, is that it protects you If something that could not be foreseen comes to light at a later date, which although the property hasn't got a problem means it isn't the right property for you. Yes, you will have lost your reservation fee, but you haven't yet been committed to losing more, such as 10% of the property price or committed to buying the property therefore you cannot be sued for the full amount or for subsequent damages.

This is a super important protection for you. As an investor I have paid many a reservation contract over the years just to find out that there was something wrong with the property, my circumstances change or that the new stadium build which would guarantee my rental income had been cancelled. Now although it doesn't feel good to lose any amount of money, it's a much better situation for you to be in, to wipe your mouth and lose that money but be grateful that it's only a small amount of money you lost as opposed to the potential 10% of the property value or worse that it could have been.

Also it is great to know that you're not going to be sued for the balance by some litigious seller; you can just lose your money and walk away. This is really where the reservation contract comes to its own, as a protection for you.

Reservation contracts are so important and reservation is a very important stage. Please do not allow any agent to try to convince you to skip it. There are some agents who will try and convince you that the reservation stage really isn't a very useful or very good protection, and you should go straight to private contract. The problem with this is a 10% of private contract is exactly what it says on the Tin, you are now paying 10% of the cost of the property which could be a huge difference to you.

The reservation fee on a 400,000 euro property, it's just 6000 euros, not a small amount of money by anybody's standards but a limited amount of money and something you can mitigate to lose. I've known somebody buy a property in the UK and easily lose double just at the reservation stage.

Whereas the 10% of fees payable at exchange of private contract on a 400,000 euros property is 40,000 euros and if at a later date you have a change of circumstances you will not be getting your 40,000 euros back.

As a bank repossession specialist, I have had a lot of clients come to me looking for bank repossessions because they were cheaper than normal real estate properties. But the real reason they were no longer able to buy normal real estate properties is because they had previously found a property which they liked, they had gone back to front and paid 10% at exchange of private contract before doing a reservation contract and then after they had paid the 10% at private contract they decided to get their ducks in a row and look for a mortgage only to find out that they could not actually get the finance which they required to buy the property. This is by the way not the mortgage advisors fault, remember the ducks in a row speech, you find your mortgage advisor and find out what level of finance you will be able to get before you go looking or pay the price which in this case was the loss of 10% of the property value.

Que the desperate scramble to raise more cash. Any cash, from anywhere. To raise enough money to keep their Spanish property dream alive, and most importantly save themselves from losing their deposit.

Sometimes with the help of liquidating assets in the UK, friends or family or a great (not good), broker this is possible. But if it is not, once the contract period has expired unless an extension is given (an act which is totally at the discretion of the seller), the property was removed from reservation and put back on the market and their 10% paid at exchange of contracts was quite rightly kept by the seller.

As I said before, there's absolutely nothing wrong with the seller doing this, it is your responsibility to make sure that you can buy the property before you pay them 10% at private contract. So even if you totally ignored my advise in chapter 4 and did not find a broker before you went viewing, I suggest that you reserve the property first, only pay a reservation fee then you find a mortgage broker sharpish, get your documents in with said mortgage broker and confirm that you can get a loan before you hand over any more of your hard earned money.

If I'm going to skip a stage of the buying process, I would personally much prefer to go from reservation straight to completion rather than skip reservation and go from 10% private contract to completion. This offers you as a buyer much more protection if it can be negotiated.

Another important thing to note is that once the 10% at private contract is paid, your agent will get paid his commission. This is why unscrupulous agents will try to get you to skip the reservation stage, from which they earn nothing and try to convince you to go straight to exchange at private contract from which they earn their commission regardless of if you actually buy the property or not. Again remember that they are working for themselves and it is in their best interests to get you to skip the reservation and go straight to exchange of contracts. I have seen this attempted on numerous occasions.

Unscrupulous people exist in every walk of life and business so what we really need to do is have the correct information to be forewarned and forearmed. I cannot emphasize this enough, I appreciate that this will not be the interesting part of this book but making a reservation protects you in as many ways as it does the seller, Going straight to private contract is a huge risk unless you know that you are a cash buyer, you already have the money secured and your circumstances will not change. You will also need to be really confident that your lawyer has done all the checks and nothing is going to come along and surprise you. (Yes, the 10% of private contract is subject to your lawyers checks but I would much prefer to have a reservation in place while that's being done. Just in case there's any dispute and my 10% of the million euro Villa I am buying, (100,000 euros paid at exchange of private contract), gets tied up in the sellers lawyers account and away from my use during a 18 month legal dispute to resolve it.

Reservation payment

The reservation fee should be sent to your lawyer. It should be paid from your bank account to your lawyers' bank account, and then from your lawyers bank account to the sellers lawyers bank account.

This is not a legal requirement and if you have a trusted Property consultant or agent then you can pay them in order to do this on your behalf but if you have not built a relationship with a property consultant or agent then follow this process to ensure that that the agent does not touch the money to avoid reservation scams

Reservation Scams

Reservation scams are where someone posing as an estate agent offers you an amazing property deal at a too good to be true price. This amazing deal and their high sales pressure tactics push you into reserving the property with no ducks in a row and paying the reservation fee directly to them to ensure that you do not miss out only to find out that the property deal never actually existed and the agent along with your money is in the wind

This also happens with rental properties so be wary

So again, unless you are using a Property consultant or a trusted Agent your reservation fee should be sent to your lawyers client account and then from your lawyers bank account to the sellers lawyers bank account, not to the real estate agent or directly to the seller. This payment process will not only protect your money but is quite important for anti money laundering reasons. Like most of Europe, Spain has very stringent anti money laundering and anti-terrorism laws and paying all monies via your solicitors client account protects you from future scrutiny.

Now just to clarify, there's nothing legally that says you cannot pay the money directly to an agent and this can be useful in some circumstances, additionally in some unusual circumstances you could even pay this money directly to the buyer. But both of these things greatly reduce your protection and could create problems for you in the future If flagged up by an audit, and sent to the department that deals with 'Blanquero de capitales' err that's money laundering to me and you. There are a couple of very quick basic checks that your lawyer should do. Along with the reservation contract, you should be presented with a 'Nota Simple' and property addresses along with some other documents which may vary depending on property and region so that your lawyer can make some very basic checks to ensure that the person selling the property is the rightful owner etc.

I recommend that you keep on thinking about it, keep on looking at the property, the area and keep on checking right up until the point of which you signed a private contract. Yes at this point searches and checks are being done by your lawyer but it will not hurt for you to keep alert and proactive in the process, making the odd double check here and there.

Top Tips for once you have found your property

- Do a reservation contract

- Do not sign a Private contract at exchange until you have your finances confirmed
- Avoid Reservation Scams

7. Your due diligence

Make sure you have a registered Lawyer

Do your due diligence. Am I starting to sound repetitive? I hope so.

I think it was Anthony Robbins who said that repetition is the mother of skill and I want you to become skilful at buying your Spanish Property. Yes you might only have to do it once, but by training and training and preparing and preparing again, when it comes to the crunch you will have the muscle memory to do it right.

Once you've made that reservation, it's really for your lawyer to start their work and do their due diligence.

When I said about getting ducks in a row, I can't emphasize enough, so I'm going to emphasize again. Please do make sure you use a qualified Spanish lawyer. It's such a strange scenario and I remember being guilty of this myself that you would come to Spain and think that things that existed in the UK or other parts of the EU just didn't exist or were not applicable in Spain.

So please be very clear. Many, many things in Spain are different from the UK. As a mortgage broker, I find the unbelievably archaic finance system in Spain to be mind blowing and very difficult for me to explain to anybody who's ever bought a property in the UK, and much, much more difficult to explain to any investor. Yes, getting certain types of finance in Spain (I mean using the Banking Mortgage products and financial instruments) is quite literally, like getting into the HG Wells time machine and going back to England in the 1850s. I kid you not.

But just like when you meet anybody from different nationalities or backgrounds. There are much more things that you have in common than you have apart and as part of the E.U the Spanish legal system is like this.

There is a Spanish Law Society. Make sure your lawyer is registered with them.

Your lawyer will do your due diligence so you need to make sure that she is competent and if they prove to be incompetent, you need to make sure you have some kind of recourse.

Unlike in the UK, here in Spain we have an intermediary that some people adopt to use to do the conveyance work on their property purchases called a Gestore. A Gestore is somewhere between an accountant and a lawyer, a bit like a book keeper. So not an accountant, and definitely not a lawyer, they sit somewhere in between.

If my hatred of people trying to cut corners and losing thousands of pounds in order to save pennies hasn't come through already please make sure that it bursts through loud and clear at this point. Do not let anybody convince you to let a Gestore do the conveyance in on your property. If you're in the UK, you would not allow a bookkeeper to do the conveyance on your property. I'm not disrespecting Gestores; they do a brilliant and essential job. Gestores can do the conveyance on your property because it is not illegal in Spain to buy property without a lawyer. They can be used to buy property successfully but due to the nature of your position as a foreign national making a massive commitment in a country where you do not know the laws or even fully know the customs, this shortcut which is usually only adopted by the Spanish who work in the industry and really know what they are doing is simply not for you.

So here are your options. You can do absolutely no conveyance on your property purchase whatsoever. That's legal and nobody involved in the selling process will be breaking the law to allow you to do it. (At least not any legal laws although they might be breaking a few moral ones).

Or you can have Jim, the guy you met down the pub, you know the same one who told you about the property you are buying and asked you to pay him the reservation fee directly because he had an off the books deal for you. Or maybe you could use the estate agent, a mate of Jims' who showed you the property that he had the second viewing on that afternoon and insisted that you skipped the reservation fee and paid the 10% at exchange of private contracts straight away? Yeah, he can do conveyance for you too. But I wouldn't advise it.

Unlike in England, where one lawyer cannot act for both the buyer and seller, In Spain, one lawyer can, as I mentioned before, do exactly that. On occasion (especially in the case of investment type deals or sales with complicated creative finance structures) this is the most practical thing to do.

But in a simple normal purchase I would always suggest to having somebody who is part of your team as this will make a lot more sense than sharing someone for the simple reason that have no conflict of interest.

So my advice is hire your own lawyer, it'll cost you roughly between 1% and 2% of the purchase price. And if you're worried about the cost, think about it like this. Compare the 1% you're paying the lawyer to the 10% or potentially 100% of the price of the property it could cost you if you didn't get one and things went wrong.

As I pointed out already, if you didn't get a lawyer and things went wrong, you will quite happily lose your 6000 reservation, and or even worse, 10% paid at exchange of private contract), which could be 15,000 euros on the cheapest of properties. And it could be even worse, you could lose all of your money if buying in cash, (let's say 150,000 euros at the lowest end going up to millions of euros at the top end), on buying a property that you later found out had serious problems which would have been picked up by a lawyer doing just the basic little bit of legal due diligence.

And most importantly, if you do use a lawyer and any of these mistakes arise due to incompetence or other issues you will be able to claim money back from their indemnity insurance which is a final but lifesaving layer of protection not offered by the Gestore, Real estate agent, Tapas bar friendly Brit or the Restaurants toilet cleaner you could have chosen as an alternative.

So is conveyance important? All together now, 'Yes it is'. With a good lawyer doing their job you are protected from any of the legal inaccuracies or aspects of a deal that even the best agent or property consultant could not possible know and would spend a great deal more time and money finding out. And as a final point as an investor for 20 years although as I have made abundantly clear many of them annoy the life out of me and all of them need to be monitored and guided to make sure that they do what you want as opposed to what they think is best, I still wouldn't buy a property anywhere in the world without one.

Top Tips for doing your Due Diligence

- Make sure that your lawyer is registered with the Spanish Law Society
- Do not Use a Gestore for conveyance
- Decide whether the deal is applicable for the same lawyer to work for both you and the Seller

8. Make a private contract

So you have made a reservation, but you still don't really know if it's the right property for you until you've had all the legal's checked out. (If I didn't labour this enough something I severely doubt please re read the previous chapter)

This is where your lawyer starts to earn his keep.

He will need some documentation before he suggested that you sign the reservation contract and as soon as that has been done his work will have started in earnest as he must now begin to perform more checks and really start earning his keep and making sure that everything is above board.

Once he has completed this 2nd layer of work and you have a firm and confident decision in principle from your Mortgage broker giving you the required confidence that you will have all of the funds required to complete, your lawyer will instruct you that you can sign the exchange at private contract and pay the 10% of the purchase price into his client account ready for its transfer to the seller.

Once signed and paid he will jump in and start the 3rd phase of his work process and begin an in depth legal due diligence to make sure that everything regarding the property you are buying is above board and in tune with the requirements of the law.

Make sure that while he is doing his job, you are still thinking and checking.

Whilst this is going on your mortgage broker and lending bank will also be hard at work and in this way the Exchange at Private contract is almost like the starter gun. Once paid all of the parties and agencies that you spent so much time to investigate and employee are now off to the races, each one working hard on your behalf to make sure that you complete your property purchase in a safe and timely manner.

Top Tips for making a Private Contract

- Make sure that the property has been reserved before you exchange at private contract
- Make sure that you are confident that you will have the monies to complete the purchase before you exchange at private contract
- If you can avoid it, do not exchange at private contract, go straight from reservation to completion.

9. Get your finances in order

As a mortgage broker myself, this is the point at which I pray
that out that of all the potential people who could be lying or
trying to trick someone in this process, the liar and the trickster is
not you.

After selling property and doing mortgages in the UK, as well as
doing them and Crete, Portugal, Cyprus and of course here in
Spain. The most disheartening aspect of my job has always been
helping someone to find a property only to later discover that
something (or often times everything) that they have told me about

their finances, (when I advise them on the kind of property they could buy in the get your ducks in a row stage), was absolute fiction.

Not knowing the truth of their finances changes everything at the due diligence stage of getting the mortgage. You might think that Spain is all Sun, Sea and Sangria or Macarena, Musica and Mañana but try getting a Spanish Underwriter to take that approach when lending out the banks money.

So I'm going to re emphasize again, please, please, please, please, please do tell your mortgage broker absolutely everything.

When you meet your mortgage broker treat him like your Catholic priest, (no, I'm not Catholic either but stay with me). You go into your Catholic priest confessional and you tell him everything. He will not judge you. He will not tempt you to call or call the police or even call them himself. He may tell you to say a few Hail Mary's but that's usually it. The same is true of your Mortgage broker and once he knows, at least he will be forearmed and forewarned with all information he needs to get your mortgage or tell you that he cannot get your mortgage, saving you all the pain and lost finance of trying to buy a property with mortgage finance that you will actually never achieve. Similarly, I would love to tell you to tell your lawyer everything. But actually I don't.

So leading directly on from the end of do your due diligence is getting your finances in order. As I said, this is the period where your mortgage broker will now start to take the very basic information you gave in your application to get your approval in principle, and flesh it out with facts and figures and proofs, in order to get you a full and final mortgage offer.

On the latter, Spanish banks really don't like giving full and final mortgage offers. (Yes we are going back to the HG Wells time machine example). Whereas in the UK, you know, you're going to get a piece of paper that says that you have an offer, it is for this much and will last for this long, well depending on the Spanish bank this may or may not be the case. I know this is very, very, unusual. So I'm going to have to ask you to trust me on this. In Spain this type of written offer can be the exception not the rule.

Quite a lot of Spanish banks will not actually ever want to give you anything in writing, they will give you a verbal agreement and just want to turn up at notary on the allotted day and sign the mortgage with you. This is super frustrating because when you're talking about getting people mortgage rates and terms, If someone turns up on the day, and there's anything different to what was agreed I will be calling Houston to report that sadly, yet again we have a problem, and you quite obviously will think that we the brokers are incompetent because it's our responsibility to get this right before Notary.

This is not me asking for your sympathy, it is our responsibility to do so. It's just a reality that you need to be made aware of. Because I've done so much business in the UK with property, it's very important to point out the differences. We could obviously only work with the banks that will give you a full and final written offer before notary and even those banks will only give you this days, definitely not weeks before. The only problem with that is that like anything in the marketplace, some of those banks, the ones who are the most efficient don't particularly have best rates or terms so this choice is a bit of a balancing act, one that your broker must take on for you and try his hardest to get right.

If (and again I have been privy to this after a 5 hour drive from the Costa del Sol to Almeria), the bank does decide to change the mortgage terms at the 11th hour, you in the worst case scenario, can just simply choose to refuse to sign because the terms were not as you were promised. You will be perfectly within your right and the bank will have to go away and rectify the scenario costing them money. I have, in this scenario seen many a 'no win or fee claim

Brit' and particularly litigious American try to claim compensation from Spanish banks for their costs of travel and hotel for this type of inconvenience and if you are ever put in this unlikely situation all I can say regarding your chances of success are, good luck with that!!!

So that's the worst case scenario that a bank can do. But in my years of being a mortgage broker, lying about your finances to you broker is the worst thing you can do to yourself (and your Spanish mortgage broker), in terms of getting your finance and getting your finances in order.

We need the information, warts and all. We need everything ugly, everything you're embarrassed about and everything you don't want to tell anybody about, we need all your deep, dark secrets, and you need to let every skeleton out of the closet. Frankly, if it relates to your finances we need to know it.

We need to know about it beforehand and package it, to make sure that it's presented in a way that the Spanish bank will accept it, or take it to a bank that will accept it as opposed to the ones that we know will not.

If we try to hide it the Spanish bank will find out about it and when the Spanish Bank find out about it they will think that not only you, but possibly we have been lying to them, and liars or people with problems with their finances and not the kind of people that they want to commit to a 20 year financial relationship with. Let me repeat that, again. People, who lie about the problems with their finances, are not the kind of people who a bank is going to want to commit to a 20 year financial relationship with.

If you tell us beforehand, we have the ability to package it, and present your case in the best light. One of the wonderful things about Spanish banks is that (Unlike in the UK), not every single case goes off to nameless, faceless underwriter who unless you're at a certain level, you have absolutely no contact with.

Spain is still a very personable 'who you know' country and we might be able to sit down and argue your case with the person able to sign off on your loan (like we could in the UK in the 1990s,) and get a result which we might not have got if your application was just a load of bits of paper sent off to a nameless, faceless underwriter somewhere in Madrid.

But if you don't tell us the truth, and their own due diligence and research, finds something that we didn't tell them, which is contrary to your application, your application is toast. And there was something that is very, very important to understand about Spanish banks, once they have declined your application there is no resurrecting it, that's the end of it.

In the UK on occasion, (when we've had very good relations with bank managers), if there was a problem, something we uncovered later in the process we could approach the local branch manager to explain, have them argued on your behalf and we could have kept the application alive at the higher levels. But once you've had a decline in Spain, that's it, 'they take you off the Barbie', you're done. You cannot go back to that bank, again, period, and your mortgage application with that bank is finished.

Now, we may be able to go and find another bank (now that we finally have the full story), you know, all the little bits that you decided to leave out and not tell us the first time?

Yes, now we have the full story, we may find out that there is another way that we can present it and we can go to another bank. But bearing in mind that the average Spanish mortgage takes six to eight weeks, you may not have six to eight weeks left on your exchange contract so you are going to have to go back to the seller, throw yourself at their feet, beg for more time so that you can get another mortgage, pray for their mercy and if they allow you to, start the whole mortgage process again. Yes again, from scratch or you are going to lose your 10% paid at exchange of private contract and the property that you spent so much time looking for and really want to buy.

Take my word for my friend, it isn't worth it. Take my word for another thing. If you've told us lies as a mortgage broker, and because your lies were found out your application was declined. It is 100% not my responsibility to magically rush through a new mortgage application with a new bank in record time in order to save you from losing your money. This doesn't mean I wouldn't try. It just means is not my responsibility to do so. It was actually your responsibility to tell me the truth at the outset.

Having covered all the things that can go wrong let me say that in 90% of the cases getting a Spanish mortgage is a very straightforward and pedestrian process.

I know I put the willies up you so you might find that hard to believe but in many aspects it really is actually quite similar to the process in the UK.

We need your financial information in three main areas.

- Proof of income/ Proof of Employment, (where your money comes from or where all your finances are going).
- Proof of expenditure, particularly returns has looked at your bank statements. (So we have proof of what comes in and how much you spend).
- And proof of your credit standing, which you know is usually from a bank or credit report in the UK and Spain. (So the bank can judge if you have managed your finances responsibly in the past)

If you're self employed or run your own business, again, you understand that in order to demonstrate your income you will need to show your 'Self Certification,' or 'Tax documents'.

So these are the simple documents we will need to start with for everybody and every bank.

Some banks will ask for more information and justifications as things progress. But once you provide all this information if you are a suitable applicant, the bank after shuffling your documents on an employee's desk for a couple of weeks (I mean really who knows what happens in that magical mystical period between submission of you documentation and the production of your mortgage offer or refusal), the documents come back out the other side of it hopefully with an offer along with certain terms.

Obviously, as a Spanish mortgage broker, I recommend that you use a mortgage broker. But actually, when I did property in the UK, I recommended using a mortgage broker there too and that's actually why I became one. You could obviously do what a lot of people do which is to go to the first bank that they find. Alternatively many take the recommendation of their real estate agent as to who can help them with a mortgage and a bad real estate agent will take them just around the corner to the closest bank to their office or the highest bidder.

Again, nothing illegal about this, nothing immoral about this and nothing wrong with this, other than the fact that you are restricting your choice.

Just like in the UK, finance options in Spain are wide and varied. The bank closest to your real estate agents office might be the bank offering the perfect deal with the best terms and conditions for you, but let's be honest, that's a one of the million chance. On the balance of probability, just like anything else, using your Spanish mortgage broker who has access to a range of banks and products suited to different financial circumstances, aims and goals will get you a much better deal.

Using your broker to 'compare the market com'; will find you a better deal with better terms for your personal circumstances and this is why it's essential to pay your Spanish mortgage broker.

Get a Broker who charges you a commission

I have this conversation a lot. Obviously, I want you to pay your mortgage broker because I am a Spanish mortgage broker and I want to get paid. But surely you also must see the common sense and logic of this?

If you say to me (like so many potential clients do), well, I know you get paid something by the bank therefore, I refused to pay you a commission you are like the example of the estate agent asking me to have the wrong motivations when looking for your mortgage deal and therefore I personally won't work with you and this is the reason why.

By not paying your broker you are re enacting the Pepa Problem. If you are telling me to get my commission from the bank, you will give me the wrong incentives. Because the incentive you're giving me is to take your case to the bank that pays me the highest commission, and the bank that pays me the highest commission may not be the bank that gives you the best deal. By telling me to get paid by the bank, you've actually made the bank my client and you my product.

Let me say that again. If you told me to get paid by the bank, you have made the bank my client, and you my product a bit like how Facebook or Instagram offers you their service for free and then makes you a product for their advertisers.

If you are paying me, then you have made sure that you are my client, and the mortgage or lending bank is the product.

Now that I'm being paid by you, it's my job to get you the best value for the money that you are paying which means defending your interests against all lenders to get you the best deal for your circumstances.

If you don't want to pay me, it is my job as a business to get me the best commission offered by a bank because as I said the bank is paying for my service. The difference to me is the loss of 1 to 2% for the mortgage loan which I may well make up or even supersede by selling your business to the highest bidder. The difference to you could be an increase in the repayment amount of your loan that could cost you tens of thousands of pounds over the 20 year term, restrictive or abusive terms and causes, high early redemption penalties and ineffective or unresponsive service from your provider.

So as in all things you pays your money you takes your choice, or in this case you don't pays your money, I takes your choice, a choice that might not be the best one for you

As such I do not work with clients who will not pay me a procurement fee for finding them a mortgage, there are plenty of brokers out there who will and you are free to do as you please. But if you do choose to use an agent who is paid only by the bank, please think of the wisdom of Pepa and at least remember what you could be getting yourself into.

A quick note on time.

Mortgages take time and yes I know that this is an annoyance but it is unfortunately a fact. Once you have found your property you like most people will just want to get on with it and get the thing bought so that you can have your first weekend away browning yourself on your terrace, and you will do, but only after the bank has done its due diligence into you and your reliability to pay back their loan.

I appreciate that with the general and well deserved mistrust of banks (think PPI, extortionate late fees payments, Bob Diamond fixing the interbank lending rate, Clauso Sueldo, IRPH, oh and then there was the little thing of a global financial crisis which led to an economic meltdown and austerity in much of the western world), it is easy to forget that they do have a genuine job to do with regards to assessing your viability for a loan. Bankings' quasi criminal recent history aside, you are asking them to lend you money, a lot of money (Most banks have a minimum loan amount so won't lend you a little bit of money on a mortgage loan), and they need to know that you are in a financial position to pay it back. This is of course only right and fair and if for any reason we forget it, a quick glance back at the global financial crisis of 2007 to 2010 which was caused when banks willfully stopped doing these exact checks in order to maximise profits should act as a sobering reminder.

So give your broker the information he needs and give the banks the appropriate time they need to look into you as a potential client and assess you. We recommend giving your mortgage broker between 6 to 8 weeks to find your finance and if nothing goes wrong it will usually be done well within this period. So please do not sign an exchange contract that legally binds you to completing on the property within 3 weeks when you have not even spoken to a mortgage broker yet.

As I always tell me clients, everything you send to me will be processed and dealt with within 48 hours but I can make no guarantees once that information hits the bank. It might be processed and approved in 7 days; it might not come out of the other end for 5 weeks. From a mortgage brokers' perspective the banking approval process is like sending your documents into

Narnia, or perhaps more like a black hole. Who knows what really goes on, on the other side?

All we can do is our regular calls and visits to chase up a case and if the risk department is looking into something that concerns them (something you neglected to tell us maybe), then the process will take longer. If the bank is short staffed due to illness the process will take longer. If your application falls during either the Christmas or the summer holiday season, the process will take longer. If your application falls anywhere between, San Juan, Semana Santa, Semana Blanca or Dia Hispaniola, the process will take longer. If you application falls on any of the regional holidays such as 'Dia de virgin Carmen 'the process will take longer and if you application falls on any of the local holidays such as other Saint days for the town that you mortgage branch is based in, I'm assuming that by now you've guessed it, the process will take longer

So as I said, all I can do is conduct myself and my business to the highest standard and chase all other parties and organizations to help you to get the results you want, I cannot perform miracles (Well actually I can but I don't like to boast and even at best I cannot perform them all the time).

So don't sign a contract that gives your broker the minimal time to get your finance. Remember that relaxed 'Mañana' lifestyle that you are so eager to buy into also applies to this process and you will need to give enough time for your application to be processed and any due diligence to be conducted in order to avoid going back to the seller and asking for more time at best paying any penalties for late completion and at worst losing your deposit for breach of contract.

As I said, some banks will give all of the funding you want and some won't but you will be advised if your mortgage has been agreed and then it's really off to the races with regards to making sure that your lawyer has arranged all of the legal's, is happy that everything is above board and in order, has done his shuffling and negotiations with the sellers lawyer and contacted your lending bank.

Buying a property anywhere is a complicated coming together to a number of moving parts but once all of these moving parts are finally working in union and your stars have all aligned we are ready for the holy grail of your Spanish property journey, Completion at Notary.

Top Tips for getting your Finances in order

- Get a mortgage broker who charges you a commission
- Tell your Mortgage Broker everything
- Get your documents ready in a timely fashion
- Make sure your exchange contract gives enough time for your broker and bank to arrange your finance

10. Come for completion

Once all of the legal checks have been completed and your mortgage has finally been approved, your lawyer will liaise with your banks and the sellers' lawyer and agree a completion date.

As previously stated all property completions in Spain take place at a Public Notary or 'Notaria' as they care called in Spain, where the Notary Public (A public servant who studies for this
position for longer than your average lawyer and is held in very high standing), will oversee the transaction of the sale scrutinizing any documentation and making sure that everybody in the deal is aware of the terms and conditions before signing in agreement to it

The public Notary system is not unique to Spain, indeed the UK used the Public Notary system many years ago and public Notaries still exist in the UK to be used for certain transactions, just no longer for buying properties and cars.

This system will seem strange but when analyzed is in fact much safer than the UK equivalent.

By still using the Public Notary system Spain ensures that your property purchase is overseen by an impartial third party, someone whose interests are neither aligned with the buyer or the seller, someone whose interests are aligned with the law, the transparency and the honesty of the transaction.

In this way the Public Notary is almost like having a Property consultant to represent your interests, make sure that you understand everything that is going on and ensure that nobody pulls the wool over your eyes, the only problem is that they come right at the end of the buying process not right at the start when you really need them.

As I previously mentioned they are impartial and represent both parties so if you were planning to pull a fast one over your seller, this is the point (if no one had realized until now), that you would be caught and sent home with you tail between your legs at best or reported to the police at worst.

Like I said being a public Notary is a position held in high regard by the Spanish and you would do well to treat them with the kind of respect that you would afford a judge when you finally get to the Notary office. After all they are the judge, they will be the judge of whether all your hard work until now results in you leaving that room the new owner of a property or not.

So once Notary is booked (or sometime before there are no hard and fast rules) you will be asked to send the remainder of your deposit funds and costs of completion, (purchase price + closing costs - reservation fee, deposit paid at exchange of contract and agreed mortgage amount already accounted for), to the account which your bank will have set up for you in the branch that will hold your mortgage.

Like most things these monies should be sent first to your solicitors client account and then transferred from her to your account at the lending bank.

For clarity I have displayed the example of a breakdown of the monies needed when buying a property. Please note that as an example I have kept the numbers simple to aid understanding;

Monies already paid of accounted for

Item	Amount in euros
Purchase price	100,000
Reservation fee paid	6,000
10% Deposit at exchange of price contracts	4,000 (+ 6000 already paid)
Agreed mortgage loan	60,000
Total accounted for	**70,000**

Monies you now need to transfer: Balance to be paid into your bank account for completion

The remainder of your deposit for the purchase	30,000
Costs of purchase Approx	
(Got taxes, Solicitor, Broker, Land registry, Notary etc)	13,000

Total now to be paid   **43,000**

If you have not done as suggested and given your lawyer a limited power of attorney to sign the mortgage deed and purchase deed on your behalf or if indeed you would like to experience the interesting event which is a completion at Notary you will need to book your flights and accommodation and prepare for what will hopefully be your last flight to Spain as a non-property owner.

Completion Day

Completion day is always a buzz. Perhaps it's the knowledge that it is the culmination of all of you work. After all of your research, building relationships with property consultants, agents, developers, lawyers, mortgage brokers and the like, your grand work is finally about to reach a conclusion. After all of this effort you are finally going to achieve your goal. We feel exactly the same way too and although these things are also important to us as agents, lawyers and brokers, after working for what can be often be up to three months on a case from start to finish we are mostly just excited about getting paid.

We are also mostly happy to finally reach completion day because buying a property in any country is a Herculean task but buying one in Spain is more like Atlas (with the world on his shoulders), than merely Hercules.

I mean buying a property is Spain involves so many moving parts; there are so many places that things could go wrong. This is even more so when one or two of the moving parts are at best inefficient or at worst untrustworthy, in these cases the fact that the sale actually makes it to Notary surprises even us.

What can you expect at Notary?

Well, busy looking self-important people who are pleasant and polite but not in the usual Spanish I don't know you but I am treating you like a long lost best friend way. The Notary will usually operate at an extremely high level of efficiency (yes you knew the Spanish were hiding it somewhere, well this is where it can usually be found). If the world really were' Divergent', the movie, all of the 'Erudite' faction would go to work in the Notary.

On the day we arrive we often meet outside to make sure that you don't get lost or intimidated inside the building.

Please do not be late, consider not only how many months' worth of work it has taken to get here but the fact that the Notary is a very busy place. Just like church weddings, if you arrive late you could miss your spot, there is another one booked right behind you.

Also please make sure that you bring the original copies of everything, I mean everything just in case. Your passport, your ID card (if you have one), your NIE card or certificate, You company Certification deeds if relevant, Do not under any circumstances fall into the trap of thinking that just because you presented them before or have emailed them to all parties that this will be sufficient for the Notary process. It is not.

The Notary is there to ensure the legality and transparency of the purchase and part of that is checking every document for authenticity. That means he needs to see your original documentation (such as your passport), pick it up, hold in his hand, look you in the face and verify that it is you. If a Power of attorney has already been signed at a Notary (so as long as the holder has their Identification and can be verified, it can be used in the process without the issuers' presence). Forgetting any of these documents is a schoolboy error which I have seen more often than you would think. It at best leads to a mad rush back to the hotel to present them in time or at worst re scheduling of the notary date to a day in the future meaning either the rebooking or flights or you having to go home empty hand and fly back again to complete the process.

Once your lawyer arrives, you will be asked to give them the originals of your documentation and she will go through and speak with the Notary clerks. Presenting documentation and making sure that everything is prepared.
She will be given the draft copy of the sales and mortgage deed which she will read through to make sure that they are correct and contain no errors.

Once everything has been agreed you will be ushered from the lounge into a boardroom looking space, some with grandiose chairs and framed pictures on the wall and others more office like (this depends on the personality of the Notary).

The table will have chairs on either side so that the buyers and their representatives can sit on one side facing the seller and their representatives on the other, with just one chair at the head of the table for the notary to, like a board room or a court yard from an ancient kingdom to remind you firmly whose court you are now in.

A lot of people do not understand the importance of a notary and how useful he is to have on your side. There are often disputes at notary (yes believe it or not after all this time and preparation), with the buyers and seller representative arguing over some point in the documentation or the deeds.

This is of course all conducted in Spanish (of course it is, we are in Spain), and although my Spanish is good, I often get lost in the minutia and idiosyncrasies of legal double speak (actually like most people I get lost in legal jargon in English too), so I do not always follow what is going on 100%. A shame really because as a professional problem solver when I do know what the problem is I can often offer a solution others have not thought of regardless to who is on the room.

My point being whatever the issue, irregularity or misunderstanding will be it is the notary's job to judge it and make a decision. Therefore it really is just like court and as such those of us with any common sense treat it as such.

Once all documents have been prepared, the notary will enter and greet us all. You will be asked to confirm your name date of birth and profession and then he will read out the deed (not the whole thing but just the most important parts of it to make sure that you understand it and explain anything that you don't.

Many Notaries will do this in English. Like most Spaniards they like to address the Brits in English because it serves as practice for the inevitable occurrence of a conversation with the next Brit they meet.

If they do not speak English then you will require a Translator. Some notaries provide them, often your solicitor can and will translate for you but in the event that this is not the case please arrange to have a translator at notary on time to confirm that you understand what you are signing.
The notary is perfectly within his rights to refuse to continue the completion if he has any reason to believe that you don't.

So once all parties have explained what they are doing, the seller and his representatives the particulars of the sale, the buyer and his representatives the particulars of the purchase, the lender the details and conditions of the mortgage, the notary exactly what you are signing and what you will be liable for, and any misunderstandings or disagreements have been ironed out, you will be asked to sign the Purchase and Mortgage deeds.

In the olden days cheques would be passed around to pay the seller, lawyer's fees, agents' fees mortgage brokers' fees etc.

This cheque exchange really was a fun part of the process but now with the stress of losing a banker's check to pay the bearer cash (if those things are even still legal in the age of anti money laundering and anti-terrorism legislation) all payments are usually conducted by the solicitor (to whom you will have transferred all of your completion monies a few days prior to the notary date), he will make the payments via bank transfer after completion.

What will still happen is that you finally get that elusive thing, the thing that just like the Hobbit in the Lord of the rings this epic journey you embarked upon was all for, yes my precious, you will get your Spanish property house keys.

With a brief smile the notary will with all the aplomb of Elvis in Vegas thank you for coming and leave the room (not the building were in his offices remember) and we are finally over the finish line.

More shaking of hands with the Sellers and their representatives and often unless anyone has an urgent appointment your whole team, agent, broker and lawyer will go for a celebratory drink at the nearest bar, a great chance for your team to build relationships if they did not know each other very well before.
A well-deserved moment of celebration after the arduous efforts to get to this point, an alcoholic pat on the back for overcoming the obstacles and a moment to relax and let it all sink in; you are finally the proud owner of a Spanish property.

Plus if you have time, have another one, so happy that he finally gets his sales commission the real estate is happy to pick up the tab, so drink up, the agent's paying.

IN SUMMARY:

THE SPANISH PROPERTY PURCHASING PROCESS

- Get your ducks in a row
- Find the property
- Get the reservation contract to your lawyer
- Send your reservation fee to your lawyer
- Make the reservation
- Due more due diligence
- Get your financial documentation to your broker
- Get any documents requested to your lawyer
- Await approval of mortgage from your broker
- Await conformation everything is in order from your lawyer
- Transfer deposit monies and costs of purchase to your lawyers client bank account
- Agree on a notary date with all parties involved in the sale
- Attend Notary with all documents requested
- Sign the mortgage and purchase deeds
- Leave notary with ownership of your new Spanish home

Top Tips for completion

- Make Sure that your completion funds are in your bank account
- Get to Notary on time
- Bring original copies of all relevant documents
- Dress Appropriately and act respectfully

11. Post completion (payments of bills and taxes)

So you have staggered out of the bar at the end of Notary Street, maybe continued the celebration with one or more of the original party and gone to get some lunch, and then what next?

Well you go to see your new property of course.

Get down to your property and make sure that everything is as agreed and expected (just in case the fully furnished apartment you bought has been stripped of everything but the kitchen sink and the light sockets)

Any problems big or small, you can still tell your agent but will now need to be logged with your solicitor as any breach of contract is a legal matter.

Hopefully this will not be the case and you can just wander around you new home, walking in and out of rooms, sitting on beds, making plans for changes and improvements and generally feeling pleased with yourself.

Yes your property purchase journey is over, enjoy it but not for too long because now the new phase of your work has just begun

Utilities

First on the list is to make sure that all utilities are connected to your apartment. The previous owner will obviously cancel all contracts so you will need to take out new contracts for water and electricity in your name. Like all utilities contracts this can take a while to organize especially if they need access to the property or you have bought bank repossession where the utilities have been disconnected for some time so get started early.

This is the reason why I said in an earlier chapter that you may as well sign a power of attorney to your lawyer or property consultant at an earlier stage as you are probably going to sign one eventually anyway. Unless you are relocating you will probably have return to the UK soon after your notary date so will not be available to call or go down to the water company, broadband or electricity supplier and open the door when they arrive if they need access to connect you.

The supply of all of these utilities require the taking out of a contract in your name which will mean in most cases giving a limited power of attorney to your lawyer in order to do so, see what I mean now. Your property management agent or property consultant can also take a limited power of attorney in your name and complete this work for a small additional fee.

Water, electricity and more importantly in the twenty first century broadband now connected you can now start the process proper of moving things around, planning rooms and buying furniture

Running costs and bills

These should have been clearly explained and outlined to you right at the outset by the selling agent and then again by your solicitor but like most things may have been tuned out into white noise under the excitement of finally finding a property you like

Well the sound on these is about to be turned right up from now on because you will have to pay them. Your bills will vary depending on the size of your property and if you leave the sprinklers on for your kids to play in or leave the air conditioning running all day so that your apartment will be nice and cool when you get home from the beach. Just like in the UK, I would not advise these actions but my real point is you pay for what you use.

The community of owners

The community of owners is a necessary evil. It is basically the equivalent of the management or service company that looks after the building which you have bought your flat in. In the UK this is farmed out to professional companies, (Like everything some are good, some are bad) and they tell you the rules and the service charge you have to pay each year.

The process is Spain is similar except the management company is made up of owners of properties in the building (or urbanizations as they are called here) as opposed to professional companies.

In accordance with the law, the owners set up a committee with a president, treasurer and other positions and as they (Spanish or foreigner), usually know very little about Spanish law they will employ a 'Community assessor', which is a company who specialize in helping this committee who know nothing, run the community which is a legal entity and as such has rules and commitments within the law.

I have not had a great relationship with some of the communities of owners I have been involved in, either personally or on behalf of my clients and the worst are usually the ones run by Brits who know the least about Spanish law and so are easily manipulated by criminal assessors who take advantage of their hubris.

Community presidents are like any other elected official, too often the ones who want the jobs are the proverbial little Hitler's who crave power and importance to hide their own ineptitude and therefore are the last ones you should give it to. As such these Presidents and easy pickings for the Criminal Assessors who can use the Presidents ego and ignorance in order to milk the community for every penny via employing service providers based on bribes and kickbacks (everything from gardeners to security), as opposed to their ability to do the job. Yes know this is a bold claim but with regards to everything I have just said in this paragraph unfortunately, I have the proof to back it up.

Luckily my experience with communities of owners is not the usual one. Most communities are as well run as an organization run by a group of novices and an administrator can be, but just like your neighbors the community of owners is a lottery. You buy a property with the sweetest old lady next door, she down sizes, leaves, is replaced by the family from hell leading to confrontations and court cases.

There is no way around this, there is no way to control it, and you can't plan for it. All you can do is buy the house you want in the area you want which is a nice neighborhood when you investigated it and hope that nothing changes. Well the same is true of communities of owners in Spain, old incompetent and bigoted Presidents will eventually retire and new competent intelligent ones will take over sacking the quasi criminal assessor and changing your experience as an owner. Or at least that is what we hope.

If you want to get involved with a community of owners please do so and I hope you experience is the complete opposite of mine. Either way every quarter when your bill comes around, as Rihanna famously said in her song, you had better have their money.

IBI and Basura

More bills just a little less contentious, IBI is an equivalent to the UK council tax and Basura means and literally is for refuse collection but the same Rihanna reference applies.

Budget for it and make sure that the monies are in the relevant accounts which have been setup by your lawyer for payment

Mortgage Payments

After all we've been through and knowing how easily a mortgage broker can lose his business due to non payments by his clients I am sure I do not need to remind you to pay your mortgage and pay it on time. And if the future prosperity of my business does not sway you then know that just like in the UK, Spain has a repossession process and persistent nonpayment will eventually lead to the repossession of your property and you will lose everything. But this is not the worst part.

The Spanish (for reasons that after 14 years living in the country I still have no idea why), have a penchant for giving unbelievably high fines which seem to bear no relation to the actual severity of the transgression committed.

As such if you think your late payment fines in the UK were outrageous, think again. I have seen 20,000 euros in fines levied by a bank in just one year for nonpayment and associated issues.

This has now begun to change as (just like the UK PPI scandal), the European courts have recently begun to take the Spanish Banks to task regarding their 'Clausos Abusivos' or Abusive Mortgage Clauses to me or you.

But for me it's too late, the scarring has been done.

My suggestion is pay your mortgage and pay it on time, trust me anything else just isn't worth the hassle.

Rental tips

If you are renting your property you have options.

With the growth of Air B&B many Buy to Let owners have dispensed with traditional rental agents but I would still advise that you have a management agent if your property is overseas, for all of the reasons I explained in the 'Getting your duck in a row section'.

You will need to register your property as a rental property with the government. Please make sure you do this as they conduct regular checks on the internet portals and if they find your property advertised for rent without being registered they can issue you with a hefty fine.

You can however do all of your marketing on the internet and many of our clients do so with great success.

Renting a property for the 'holiday lets' market will require some specifics;

You will need a good cleaner who is reliable and can work to the schedule of your changeovers

You will need a maintenance person because if your clients arrive for their holiday to a leaky sink or no air con you are getting a bad review which could lead to loss of future business and if they cannot use the apartment at all you may have to refund them their money.

A welcome pack is a great way to greet your clients

Have a document for the apartment with information of the area, what to do there and most importantly how everything works or suffer the 3am phone call when they cannot turn the oven on, (and trust me you will be too tired after being woken from your deep sleep to ask why they want a pizza at that time)

The best part of a rental business is that it grows over time and repeat customers are your bread and butter so treat them well, be organized go above and beyond the call of duty and your rental property will be a fully-fledged repeat business concern within a matter of years.

Top Tips for Post completion

- Get your lawyer to connect Utilities with their Power of Attorney
- Set up direct debits for payments of Utilities, taxes, mortgage and Community fees
- Get a Management agent to look after your property regardless of if you intend to rent it out of not
- Get a Rental agent if you plan to rent it out and sign up the property up with the Junta to avoid fines for renting illegally

12. Summary

Phew finally we made it.

I sincerely hope that you have enjoyed this book

I hope that the erratic scatter gun style of writing has not stopped you from getting the important information I am trying to convey.

When I meet holiday makers I always ask them if they enjoyed their stay, strange as it seems I feel proud if they have enjoyed their time in my adopted country, the country where I have made my home and I feel sad and responsible if they don't.

This is multiplied 10 fold when considering the purchasing process.

I really want you to have a happy and stress free experience when buying a property in Spain. I know after reading this book it might seem impossible but I promise you, armed with the information contained in this book and right people at your side none of these cautionary tales will apply to you.

I really want you to get the property that you want.

I really really want you to get good value and not lose money along the way.

I really, really, really want you to get good service, to be taken care of and protected during the process.

I want this because anything else leaves me feeling ashamed of my profession and disappointed in my peers. Anything less will leave me ashamed of the country and its systems that I left the country of my birth to make my home.

So if you are just starting your journey please use this book to whatever advantage it can give you and if you would like some help getting the best from your real estate agent, lawyer, broker and avoiding the pitfalls or being blown up by the mines in the minefield that is buying a Spanish property, get in touch and I would be happy to help you.

Want more information? Find us on Social Media

 www.puor.co.uk

 www.linkedin.com/in/felix-joseph-781a893

 @YOURPUOR

 @felixpuor

 @propertyunder1

Felix Joseph

About the Author

I have worked in the Property Investment and financial services field for over 20 years as a successful Investor, Mortgage broker, Property Mentor, Trainer and Writer, building a mixed type personal portfolio in the UK, Spain, Portugal and Cyprus along the way.

Property Under One Roof has never tried to be a Real Estate or Mortgage company. We started selling properties we had sourced for ourselves because as the old adage goes, 'you can't buy them all'. Similarly we started doing mortgages out of the necessity to build the relationships with banks we needed to get the deals and terms we wanted for our own deals and then soon found that we were in a position to pass this benefit on.

Having semi retired and relocated to Southern Spain on Passive Income I replicated the process in Spain not only surviving the recession but growing our business by founding the Spanish Bank Repossession Co op in 2014 which allowed us to work with Spanish Bank Repossessions and hedge funds to get our clients access to the best deals available.

As the recent dramatic change in world economic circumstances look set to herald a new environment of opportunity for those buying Spanish property and We look forward to helping our clients access there through Obtaining them Spanish bank finance, Property Consultancy and Joint venture Projects

Why I wrote this book

As a bank repossession specialist about a 3rd of my clients came from people who had tried to buy a normal property in Spain (via the real estate process) and had been taken in by an unscrupulous estate agent, misinformed, misadvised, not protected by lawyers who did their job (which in their mind is following the law and not the protection of their client), lost over 10% of the purchase price often between 30 and 80,000 euro), and were then left looking at buying a knockdown price Spanish bank repossession property as the only hope of keeping their Spanish property dream alive, (which is in fact by researching Spanish bank repossession properties is how they found me).

One day I began to think If only I had got to them sooner, if only I met them before they started rather than at the end of their property journey. I know I could have helped them to buy that property safely. I know I could have saved them the loss of tens of thousands of pounds. I know I could have saved them life-changing and life challenging amounts of stress and been paid handsomely for my efforts. It is these true stories which inspired the writing of this book.

Printed in Great Britain
by Amazon

47654273R00071